Giving Thanks
The Art of Tithing

By Paula Langguth Ryan

Pellingham Casper Communications, LLC
How-To Publications That Make A Difference
1121 Annapolis Road, Suite 120
Odenton, MD 21113

Publisher's Cataloging-in-Publication
(Provided by Quality Books, Inc.)
Langguth Ryan, Paula
Giving thanks : the art of tithing/ by Paula Langguth Ryan.
p. cm.
ISBN 1-889605-07-7
1. Success — Religious aspects.
2. Wealth — Religious aspects. I. Title
BJ1611.2.L36 2004   204'.46
QBI04-200269

Pellingham Casper books are available for special promotions and
premiums. For details, contact: Director, Special Markets
800/507-9244

First Edition - 2005

Printed in the United States of America

Photo By Stephanie Wooton
Hair and Makeup By Shirley Proctor Studios

Giving Thanks
The Art of Tithing

By Paula Langguth Ryan

Pellingham Casper
Baltimore

Other Pellingham Casper prosperity tools
by Paula Langguth Ryan:

Bounce Back From Bankruptcy:
A Step-By-Step Guide to Getting Back on Your Financial Feet

Feng Shui Bagua Treasure Mapping Playkit

The Art of Abundance Electronic Newsletter
(www.ArtOfAbundance.com)

21 Days to a More Abundant Life
Break the Debt Cycle—For Good!
Embracing Your Abundance
Expanding Your Container
How to Create Supercharged Intentions that Effortlessly Manifest
How to Manifest a Debt-Free and Prosperous Life
How to Manifest the Right and Perfect Job
How to Manifest the Right and Perfect Mate
Reversing Financial Adversity
The Truth About Giving & Receiving
Heal Your Relationship With Money

For more information about these products and Paula's
keynote, workshops, lectures, training and coaching services, visit http://www.ArtOfAbundance.com

Prologue

How much abundance can you visualize coming into your life—realistically—in the next year? How about in the next 30 days? Do you base your answer strictly on the amount you *know* may come into your life from your paycheck, clients, tax refunds, consumer rebates, inheritances and the like? Or do you base your answer on your faith in what you desire?

A single mother called and left me a breathless message two days after attending my prosperity seminar. She spoke so quickly, the message sounded like Alvin and the Chipmunks had called: *"Paula, I wanted to tell you about an AMAZING prosperity story that happened to me, and I REALLY want you to call me back, so I can share this AMAZING PROSPERITY STORY with you!"*

It was nearly midnight, so instead of calling, I made a detour to my study. At every workshop, I teach people the truth about tithing and then I give everyone a blank postcard and ask them to write on it something they want to manifest in their lives during the next 30 days.

Some people write their desires for stronger relationships, physical healing, freedom from fear, increased prosperity in some form or another. This woman had written a single dollar figure on her postcard: $10,000. I went to bed and woke up the next morning fairly "sizzling with zeal and anticipation," as Charles Fillmore would say, eager to hear this woman's amazing prosperity story.

When she arrived home from work Monday evening, she

opened her mail. Enclosed in one envelope was a completely unexpected check for $8,000. We laughed and said she had another 18 days to manifest the additional $2,000.

How was this manifestation of a completely unexpected $8,000 possible? Because this woman had learned how to get herself and her limited thinking out of the way so she could be in the flow—the divine flow, that is.

Once she put herself in the prospering flow of abundance—tithing on every level of her life, including her thoughts, words, actions and treasures—she manifested exactly what she desired within 48 hours of setting her intention.

Once you discover how to do the same, nothing can stand in your way of creating the life you truly desire.

> Paula Langguth Ryan
> Carolina Beach, NC
> February 5, 2005

Table of Contents

Foreward, by Catherine Ponder   14
INTRODUCTION   15

CHAPTER ONE:
In the Beginning   21
What Exactly Is a Tithe?   22
Misconceptions About Tithing   28
The Truth About Tithing   30
The Natural Benefits of Tithing   34

CHAPTER TWO:
Tapping Into the Spiritual Flow   43
Meeting Your Every Need   46
The True, Divine Model of Supply and Demand   52

CHAPTER THREE:
Is It Possible That More Good Exists For You?   61
Is Your Glass Half Empty or Half Full?   63
Getting Started Tithing   65
Where Should You Tithe?   68
The Mechanics of Tithing   72
What's Stopping You From Tithing?   74
What "Can't Afford" & "Costs Too Much" Mean   78

CHAPTER FOUR:
Becoming One With Life's Prosperous Flow   81
A Multitude of Blessings   86
Freeing Up Your Trapped Prosperity   89
Letting Go of Your Guilt Gifts   91
Practicing the Art of Unconditional Releasing   95

CHAPTER FIVE: Practicing Acts of Courage   97
Embracing Impermanence   101
Projecting an Aura of Abundance   104

CHAPTER SIX: Discovering Your Intentions   111
Aligning Your Actions With Your Intentions   113
Releasing Control   120
Finding the Freedom in Forgiveness   125

CHAPTER SEVEN: The Etiquette of Tithing   131
Staying in the Constant Flow   134
The Art of Receiving   138
Setting Your Intentions   141
Following Your Life Purpose/Releasing Fear   143
Relationships   145
Debt Free and Prosperous Living   146
Transitions   148
Career/Business   149
Health and Vitality   150

CHAPTER EIGHT:
Expanding Your View of Prosperity · **153**

Honor Yourself Enough to Stay the Course · 157
Measuring Your Success · 168
Don't Forget to Breathe! · 172

Epilogue · **175**

"If the only prayer you ever say
is 'thank you', it will suffice."
— *Meister Eckhart*

This book contain references to God. I understand that some readers might be uncomfortable with the word God, and I invite you to substitute Source, Universe, Universal Energy, Great Spirit, Science, Goddess, or whatever else you feel comfortable calling the unexplained energy that swirls among us and created such wonders as human beings, a dragonfly and the waves.

Dedication

To everyone, everywhere, whose life has
ever touched mine. You helped me prosper
and grow in untold ways, and I dedicate this
book to you, with all my thanks. Thank you
for feeding my spirit and for allowing me to
feed yours.

Acknowledgements

First and foremost, I thank God—the God of My Understanding—for all the incredible gifts in my life, especially the gift of courage. You were right: I'm not sure I *do* have a big enough container to hold it all, but day by day with Your help I'm learning to *be* a bigger container.

As always, an entire community helped support my work and this project with tithes of their time, talent, treasures and spirit. My eternal gratitude to: Refik Agri, Sue Bailey, Linda Damesyn, Robert Drake, Janet and Robbie Hall, Nellie Lauth, April J. May, Luanne McKenna, Kathy Miller, Kaye and Jervais Phillips, Debra Proctor, Shirley Proctor, Marty Ward and Ted Zeiders. If I've overlooked anyone, it's not for lack of love.

I offer my heartfelt thanks to my coaching clients, students, newsletter subscribers, readers and others who have sought answers to their questions about how we can learn to accept our divine birthright of Universal Abundance. Your questions were as valuable to me as your more tangible support.

Special thanks to my original Monday night prosperity class (hugs to Anita, Amy, April, Edith, Linda, Mary and Pat) for being such willing guinea pigs, for trusting the process and for all your love and support.

Immense gratitude and love to Debra Proctor for seeing the vision of this book made manifest and for providing me with the sanctuary and the silence in which it was written.

A big woof of thanks (again) to my fellow spiritual traveler Linda Damesyn for being the best friend, dancing buddy and dog-sitter a girl could ever ask for.

My unending love and appreciation goes to April J. May for being a willing student, for believing in my work without fail and for being the most enthusiastic voluntary publicist in the world.

I'm deeply grateful, to Shirley Proctor--for her tireless and enthusiastic editing; any errors in punctuation are a reflection of my stubbornness--not her skills. Many thanks to Ravi Subramanian for his crackerjack proofreading skills and and Kristelle Sim for her editorial suggestions.

Special thanks to Rev. Catherine Ponder for introducing me to the art of tithing and for graciously writing the Foreward to this book; to Rev. Judith Elia Brosius Ballard for being my first prosperity penpal and for becoming my treasured friend; to Beth Kaufman for teaching me the importance of living an authentic life; to Kaye Phillips for reminding me that nothing is ever truly lost or destroyed; and to Nellie Lauth, for just being.

Thank you all for being exactly who you are.

- Paula Langguth Ryan

The word "tithe" means "tenth" and since ancient times all great civilizations have taught the power of caring and sharing through the act of tithing a tenth of one's income at the point or points where one is being inspired.

Tithing has been described as "the permanent road to prosperity." I began tithing fifty years ago at a time when a tenth of my weekly income was $2.50.

This simple, weekly act brought gradual increase over the years. Tithing is not "a get rich quick scheme." It is a universal law endorsed by our Creator to help humankind prosper and succeed on all levels of life.

Of all the prosperity laws I have researched and written about in sixteen (16) books, I receive more mail about the tithing law of prosperity than all the others combined! People are hungry to know of this divine and permanent law of prosperity.

So I invite you to join countless people worldwide as you "tithe and thrive." This book shows you how!

Catherine Ponder
author, *Dynamic Laws of Prosperity*

Introduction

When I was a young girl, I used to spend my summers grandma-sitting my great-grandmother on her farm in northern Indiana. One of my favorite morning activities was harvesting the raspberries from the raspberry canes. Each morning I'd go out with my little basket and I'd come back into the farmhouse kitchen with at least two pints of raspberries. One pint, we'd clean and put in the freezer; the other pint, I'd sprinkle sugar on and eat for breakfast. I was amazed that every morning there were always at least two pints of raspberries waiting to be picked.

One summer it dawned on me that since there were two pints of raspberries to pick every day, I could save a lot of time and energy if I picked the raspberries once a week. That way, I could harvest all fourteen pints of raspberries at one time.

A week passed and I ran to the raspberry patch and began harvesting my raspberries with great joy. When I finished, instead of the fourteen pints of raspberries I had anticipated, I still had only two pints. I couldn't understand what had happened. There should have been seven times as many raspberries, but there weren't!

Many years later, I understood what had happened that summer. As long as I was embracing my abundant supply of raspberries every day and giving thanks for that abundance through my willingness to pick my daily raspberries, my abundance continued. It was only when I stopped systematically giving thanks for my abundance that the flow of abundance decreased.

Because I didn't show up to harvest my raspberries on a daily basis—because I didn't give thanks for the good I was already receiving—the abundant flow of raspberries passed me by.

Some raspberries ripened and fell to the ground or were eaten by birds. Other raspberries simply didn't develop, because there was still an abundant supply on the canes that hadn't been harvested. Because I stopped giving thanks for the harvest of two pints of raspberries every day, God figured I wouldn't be happy with fourteen pints a week, either.

That was when I understood part of the Divine Law of Prosperity: *Until you learn to be happy with what you have, you won't be happy with more.*

Until we learn to notice and cheerfully embrace the abundance that surrounds us right now—whether it be money, ideas, people or opportunities—and give thanks for that abundance by giving back of our time, our talents and our treasures, we won't be open and receptive to additional abundance.

Giving Thanks: The Art of Tithing is designed to help you more fully understand how to tap into your innate abundance, using the core prosperity principle of tithing. Tithing is an ancient prosperity technique that puts you directly in the flow of Universal Energy and Abundance.

This is the true nature and power of tithing. Tithing isn't a financial transaction, although sometimes tithing involves giving and receiving financially. True tithing is so much deeper than money alone. The art of tithing helps you open up to greater good in all areas of your life. True tithing creates an expansion of yourself. It is a tool that helps you be more of who you truly are, have more of what you truly desire and do more of what you truly love.

Tithing is about cultivating gratitude and thankfulness. It's about giving thanks for what God, Jehovah, Universal Spirit or Infinite Intelligence has already given you. By giving thanks with everything you are, everything you have, everything you give and everything you receive, you open the flow of abundance to you and draw to you even greater good than that which you send out. True tithing is a prayer of thanksgiving offered up in acknowledgement of God's good.

I will be the first to admit that this book is not for everyone. In fact, this book may not be for most people. This book is only for people who are strong enough, courageous enough and motivated enough to take the first step toward letting go of the illusion that the abundance in their lives comes from themselves, their jobs, their spouse's income, their disability or unemployment checks, their parents' financial assistance or the lottery.

This book is for people who are willing to set aside—even temporarily—any fears or objctions that arise from their concept of God. Whatever name you give to the expansive power from which our world sprang forth, there is one immutable truth: There is only one power and one presence in the Universe, a power that is only good, and from which everything in life unfolds, in Divine Order, for our highest good.

This book is for people who are strong enough, courageous enough and trusting enough to allow this truth to unfold in their lives and to embrace this truth, no matter how it may appear.

This book is for people who are strong enough, courageous enough and secure enough to set aside their skepticism and their current beliefs about what they know about tithing to see the true meaning of the action behind the word. Only by your willingness to have an open mind will it be possible for you to fully embrace the original intent of the principle of tithing.

So how do we learn to embrace the abundance that we do have? How do we learn to give thanks for everything that occurs in our lives, so we can learn to recognize and receive all the good that flows into our lives? How do we get past the obstacles, explanations, excuses and fears that keep us from giving and receiving thanks—willingly, cheerfully and joyfully—every day? I hope by the time you finish reading this book, you will know these answers for yourself.

Each of us has our own issues around giving and receiving that we need to heal. The first step for many of us, when learning to give thanks, is learning to be open and accepting *receivers*. Fortunately, just as we've been conditioned NOT to receive, we can recondition ourselves to willingly receive everything that comes into our lives, even things we've designated as undesirable or disastrous.

For instance, I used to live in the boondocks about forty-five minutes from everything and occasionally I got stuck behind a slow-moving vehicle. Now, I could choose to spend my time and energy trying to get around the slowpoke. I could try to race past him when we came to a town where the road became two lanes. I could fuss and fume and make my blood pressure go up over the fact that I was going to be late. Or I could choose to assume that this condition, this slow-moving vehicle, had been placed in my path for a reason.

I could choose to receive this gift and give thanks for it, even though I might not be able to see *how* it might be for my highest good. The possibilities for good in our life are limited only by the limits of our imagination and the limits of our ability to receive.

Maybe if I'd been going faster I would have been involved in the accident whose aftermath I passed on the road a few minutes later. Or maybe I'd been running all week in such high gear that this was a gift from the Universe, allowing me to slow down a bit and get centered. When we actively change the way we view the events in our lives—when we can think of them not as good events or bad events, but as just events—we get in sync with the universal energy that contains limitless abundance.

When we stop trying to control the outcome of events we demonstrate our willingness to let God reveal our abundance to us in the form it's supposed to take, even if that form is one that we don't initially recognize as being for our highest good. As a result, our abundance increases dramatically.

There is only one thing we can truly control: our reactions to our thoughts. If something disturbs you, stop adding it to your consciousness. If the news makes you worried and anxious, turn off the television or radio, cancel the newspaper. Stop focusing on what's not working in your life and start focusing on what *is* working.

We each have so much abundance in our lives, but most of us can't see it because it's not taking a form we recognize. We have our sights so set on abundance being a specific thing, like a raise or a bigger house or peace, that we don't see the true abundance. And until we see the true abundance, embrace it and give thanks for it, we won't be in alignment with the greater abundance that's contained in the universal energy that surrounds us.

Over time you will begin to notice how all the events in your life are important steps toward your permanent prosperity. They are all part of your Universal or Divine Plan, *your* life's purpose. They are all unfolding in Divine Timing, according to Divine Law.

As your perception toward abundance begins to shift, you will also begin to unconditionally give thanks for those events without even thinking about it. When you open your mind and heart to freely receive the limitless abundance that God has available for you, you will find every area of your life improving. This is my greatest hope for you. It is why I wrote this book.

There is so much abundance swirling around each of our lives right now that no one has yet built a container large enough to hold it all. Until you actively take the theory of gratitude and put it into practice through the art of tithing, you—like most people—will never experience even a fraction of that abundance.

If you are ready to embrace your abundance, then I invite you to join me in a most incredible adventure as you learn how to put the art of tithing to work in your life, starting today!

Chapter One: In the Beginning

A grateful mind is a great mind,
which eventually attracts to itself great things.

— Plato

Every culture and every religion from the beginning of time understood that our abundance was a gift and that we were somehow stewards of those gifts. Arabians, Babylonians, Buddhists, Chinese, Christians, Egyptians, Greeks, Hindus, American Indian, Jews, Muslims, Pagans, Persians, Phoenicians, Romans—every sect and every group—understood the spiritual basis of the ancient Divine Law of Prosperity.

People from ancient cultures understood that their mind, body, soul—every possession and every idea they had—were instruments or channels of their abundance, which came from whatever name they gave to Universal Spirit. This is clear from Egyptian hieroglyphics and Babylonian cuneiform tablets, as well as early Greek and Roman writings. Ancient Romans, for example, poured the first wine from each year's harvest onto the ground before taking a sip themselves, giving back the first portion to Mother Nature, whom they believed had graciously given it to them.

People everywhere have always searched for a way to consistently stay in touch with their divinely inspired flow of abundance. To accomplish this, they followed two primary principles regarding their abundance. First, they consistently

21

gave forth the first portion of what they were given, to honor the Source of all their good. Second, they gave this portion to wherever or whomever spiritually fed, helped or inspired them.

Before tithing was ever recorded in writing, it was handed down from generation to generation and understood as the Divine Law of Prosperity. Tithing was seen for what it was: an action to be taken in order to give thanks for the abundance that had already manifested, and to give thanks in advance for the greater good that was yet to come.

What Exactly Is a Tithe?

Honor the Lord with thy substance,
and with the firstfruits of all thine increase.
— The Bible, Book of Proverbs (3:9)

Tithing is about saying "thank you," which always begins with putting some gratitude in our attitude. Giving thanks is about tithing not only with our money, but also with our thoughts, words, actions, time, efforts and possessions.

Tithe from your thoughts: Give thanks to everyone who comes into your life for the role they play in your life, whether it was a role you welcomed or not.

Tithe from your words: Speak words of love, gratitude and thanksgiving rather than criticism, condemnation and sarcasm.

Tithe from your actions: Act with integrity, honesty and courage rather than fear.

Tithe from your time: Volunteer; go out of your way to

stop and help someone in need; truly listen when a child is speaking.

Tithe from your efforts: Approach everything you do with gratitude and joy, even if it's not what you truly desire to be doing at that moment.

Tithe from your possessions: Give some of what you own to others, without expecting anything in return.

How and Why Tithing Works

People always ask me to explain why tithing works. You know the saying "you get more flies with honey than vinegar?" Have you ever noticed that when you smile at people you meet you are likely to get a smile in return? We are constantly sending either positive or negative energy into the universe. That energy is constantly multiplied and returned to us in kind. Tithing works like a magnetic force, attracting good. If your magnetic force is negative, it will repel your good instead of attract it.

Tithing provides us with a proven, systematic way to multiply our good through a demonstration of our willingness to give back one-tenth of everything we've been given. We tithe as a show of gratitude for what we have already been given and as a symbol of our gratitude for and faith in the fact that even greater good is coming to us. Tithing is a way of showing that we are ready, willing and able to embrace that increased abundance. Tithing is a nonverbal way to say we are ready to have omnipresent abundance manifest in our lives now.

The word *tithe* is based on the word *tenth*. It is a percentage.

Ancient cultures believed that the number ten was a powerful number of increase, symbolic of the whole. Everything begins and ends with ten. We count to ten, and then begin again, adding one to the next tenth. Computer languages are written with two binary numbers: 1 and 0. The number 1 reaffirms the Universal Truth that we are all One. We are all interconnected with God, the Universe, Spirit. This connection is furthered by 0, which shows how there is no beginning and no ending, but only an eternal natural and spiritual cycle.

When you give thanks for what God has provided you, by selflessly giving back one-tenth of what you've been given, you connect yourself to this cyclical flow and your blessings are multiplied tenfold, even hundredfold. When you are connected to this flow, your tithe increases your service to others, which in turn increases the supply of abundance in your life.

Historically, tithing was considered an act of service and giving the tenth part, or the tithe, was an honorable action. The biblical story of Jacob illustrates the honor of tithing. When Jacob was a young man, he set off from home to find fame and fortune. One night during his journey, he awakened from a dream in which he saw himself being blessed by God. He was so overwhelmed with gratitude that he immediately built a monument to God.

Then he made known the blessings he desired: He asked for financial prosperity, guidance, peace of mind and reconciliation with his family. He vowed in good faith to give God a tithe or one-tenth of everything that he was given, without even knowing whether or not God would provide these blessings. Jacob went on to become one of the Bible's early millionaires and within twenty years had realized these blessings.

Jacob understood that tithing was an exercise in faith; a way of giving thanks in advance for the good that would come to him, without any expectation that this good would actually appear.

Tithing doesn't work just because you've given a tenth of your income to your church or temple. Too many people have approached tithing with the mindset that tithing is a duty or obligation. They've had an expectation that they would get something in return if they fulfilled this obligation.

Tithing is not about giving back to God out of duty, obedience or necessity, or giving in order to get something in return. Tithing is not about money, and it's not a religious injunction created by the Judeo-Christian religions. Tithing actually predates the Bible by centuries and has been practiced in various forms by all cultures.

Many cultures, wanting their people to be ever prospered, went so far as to make tithing a requirement. The giving of the tithe was written down in a specific legalistic form in the Talmud, the Jewish law, which also forms the first five books of today's Bible. The various written laws created intense debate over what should be tithed, how much and to whom. Questions regarding the particulars of tithing laws still arise today among Talmudic scholars—and among Christian scholars, who debate whether or not the laws of tithing pertain to members of their faith.

Somewhere along the way the intent of the law, the Spirit of the law, was lost. This is why Jesus stated that he came not to destroy the law, but to fulfill it. His purpose was to remind people of the Spirit of the law rather than the letter of the law.

25

Jesus recognized that the Spirit of the law was often being overlooked, and he sought to inspire people to embrace their personal connection to Spirit. That is why he provided a simplified version of all the commandments and laws:

1. You should love God—the God of your Creation, the God of your Being, the God of your Understanding—with all your heart, soul and mind.

2. You should love your neighbor as yourself.

He also sought to remind people that the tithe was not intended to be viewed as an obligation, or a duty, or an act of obedience. The tithe was intended to be given willingly, cheerfully and joyfully as a love offering, a glad tiding. This is why the Christian biblical texts refer to tithing as a free-will offering. Your tithe was to be given of your own free will, not out of any sense of duty or obligation. Right here and now, I hope to put to rest an enduring myth about tithing being an obligation. The truth is, you do not have an *obligation* to tithe— you have an *opportunity* to tithe.

Story after story abounds of those who gave obligatory tithes but who were not blessed, because their tithe was given routinely, with no thought toward gratitude or thanksgiving. Tithing became a household chore, and people routinely gave of the first and the best of all they had. They brought their tithes to the temples and had great feasts, and gave their tithes to the priests to be used by them to help feed others, both spiritually and literally. But more and more, the tithe was seen as just another obligation, not as an opportunity to give thanks.

26

Whether you call it a glad offering, a free-will offering, a heave offering, a love offering, or by any other name, a tithe is, was, and forever more shall be, intended as an offering of thanksgiving. When you begin to give freely, and release your need to control the outcome of how your good will be returned to you, you make it possible for that good to appear. Let me illustrate this with a quick story (you will find this book peppered with stories like this one):

> A songwriter found herself in the red financially. Several clients owed her money. Rather than spend her time and energy worrying about what she didn't have, she affirmed that *"The Universe will take care of me. It always does. I'm sick of worrying."*
>
> She went to her post office where she discovered a check from a musician to whom she had gifted one of her songs to record. She had given her song freely—without asking for any royalty—because she knew the musician would create a beautiful rendition of it.
>
> Her good was multiplied and returned to her in an unexpected way.

This woman discovered that tithing takes many forms, but has one common theme: A tithe is something you give to another without any expectation of anything in return. In the case of tithes, size doesn't matter; intent does.

Misconceptions About Tithing

A mind once stretched by a new idea
can never go back to its original dimensions.
– Oliver Wendell Holmes

People are often confused about tithing, based on misconceptions they grew up believing. Hopefully, this section will help clear up some of that confusion. Let's start by looking at what tithing is *not*.

Tithing is not about giving money to spiritual leaders, although tithes should always be given to those who provide you with spiritual help or feed your spirit with inspiration and joy. This could be your local church, temple, mosque or synagogue, an inspirational writer, speaker or musician or elsewhere.

Tithing is not about bribing God in order to get more abundance. Tithing is not about the gifts that we will gain in return. The idea that it is better to give than to receive has merit but presents a peculiar paradox. For it is in the giving that we receive greater abundance in all areas of our lives.

Many people think of tithing as a way to give in order to get something in return. Obedience. Duty. A requirement. A way to avoid disappointing God. Tithing is none of these things.

Tithing is like breathing. You can hold your breath anytime you want. You can hold your breath until you turn blue and pass out. Then the natural rhythm of breathing will take over unconsciously. You'll begin giving and receiving air, in and out, whether you want to or not.

Becoming aware of how you unconsciously breathe or

hold your breath in times of stress can help you create greater health in your life. The same is true with tithing. Becoming aware of the ways you unconsciously tithe or withhold your tithe, will help you create greater abundance in your life.

You can withhold your tithe anytime you want, but your tithe will be paid somewhere, somehow. The natural law of giving and receiving demands it, because there is a Spiritual or Cosmic cause to every effect. You can consciously give thanks to the places that feed your spirit, or you can unconsciously give to the places that deplete your spirit. When you don't tithe to your spiritual Source, you wind up tithing elsewhere.

> A woman tithed and saved $417 on auto parts. Another woman tithed and received a lower mortgage rate than the one she had locked into. A man tithed and he lost weight, thereby alleviating health problems.
> A woman withheld her tithe and her purse was stolen. After years of tithing and building a prosperous business, a man decided to bargain with God and withhold his tithe. The following year his business fell into financial ruin. A woman tithed regularly to a place that no longer fed her spirit, and was unable to break free from persistent financial difficulties.

Tithing offers you an incredible opportunity to take control of your future by letting go of and giving back a portion of what you've been given. This is the paradox of tithing. The only way to control your future abundance is to relinqiush control of a portion of your current abundance. The choice is up to you. You can choose whether you want to be aware and conscious of the circulation in your life or not. You can choose to actively make things happen in your life or passively allow them to happen. Remember: There is no obligation to tithe. There is only an opportunity to tithe. What you do with that opportunity is up to you.

The Truth About Tithing

The greater the truth to be expressed,
the more simply can it (and should it) be clothed.
— H. Emilie Cady

In its truest form, tithing is simply a way of saying "thank you" for the abundance that is manifesting or appearing in your life today and in the days to come. Walter Russell said, "All knowledge can be obtained from the Universal Source of All Knowledge by becoming One with that Source."

Tithing is an acknowledgement that we *are* One with that Source. Tithing is a way of giving thanks in advance for the greater good that is about to come to you. Tithing is about giving thanks for the past and for the future. Tithing plops you squarely down in the flow of abundance. The practice of tithing involves giving back a percentage—one-tenth or 10%—of what you've been given, to places that feed your soul spiritually.

The Divine Law of Prosperity, which includes the principle of tithing, is a universal, immutable, eternal Truth. The Divine Law of Prosperity is governed by order and harmony and is a law in the same way the Law of Gravity is a law. The Divine Law of Prosperity follows all the rules of physics:

1. An object in motion tends to stay in motion unless it is acted upon by an equal, opposite force.

2. An object at rest tends to stay at rest unless it is acted upon by an outside force greater than itself.

Likewise, your abundance continues to grow unless it is stopped by a force that is equal to and opposite itself. Your abundance grows in direct proportion to your giving and gratitude.

Gravity did not begin at the point when Isaac Newton got bonked on the head with an apple or at the point when he calculated and wrote down the equations that make up the Law of Gravity. Nor did tithing begin when it was first recorded in the Bible or when it was set down as a law in the Mosaic Covenant or whenever you first learned about tithing. The prospering power of tithing, like the grounding force of gravity, has existed from time immemorial.

The effects of tithing, like the effects of gravity, do not occur because we make it so or because we recognize its existence. Gravity does not cease to exist when you enter an anti-gravity chamber or sail off in a rocket into outer space. In these instances, all you have done is stopped the Law of Gravity from having any influence in your life at that moment. The pull of gravity still exists and is still at work in your life, whether you are physically present in a gravitational field or not. The prospering power of tithing still exists and is still at work whether or not you have physically placed yourself in the flow of abundance. The only thing that changes, if you decide not to tithe, is the strength of the law's effect on your life.

The Law of Geometry is another example of a universal law in action. What do you know about triangles? The sum of the angles of any triangle will always equal two right angles, or 180 degrees. You can draw any triangle, and before you put pen to paper, I can tell you with *absolute certainty* that the sum of all three angles will equal 180 degrees. Get out your paper and pen and protractor and I'll wait while you draw a gazillion triangles, if—like me—you need to prove this theorem for yourself.

> *Everything that is freely given with thanks*
> *will be multiplied and returned to you*
> *in expected and unexpected ways.*
> — The Divine Law Of Prosperity

You may have already known that the sum of the angles of a triangle always equals 180 degrees, or you may have just learned this fact from me. Your knowing it or not knowing it does not make it any more or less true. This law was true even before anyone recognized it. It is true today. It will be true forevermore, because it is based on an immutable or unchangeable law.

These laws are everlasting, like sunshine. The sun is always shining. The rotation of the earth does not cause the sun to stop shining. The passage of a cloud in front of the sun does not stop it from shining. Even if we are in some dark, windowless basement or prison cell, far removed from any source of light, the sun does not stop shining. We may gain no comfort or joy from the sunshine in these instances—the sun may not be shining on *us*—but the sun itself never stops shining.

So it is with our blessings, when we remove ourselves from the Universal flow or source of those blessings. When we cease to give thanks for what we have received, we remove ourselves from the influence of the Divine Law of Prosperity: we remove ourselves from the benefits of tithing. The Divine Law of Prosperity still exists, and our blessings are still being poured out, but we are not present to receive them.

Only two things can stand in the way of having the unlimited supply that the Universe has available for us. The first is our own ignorance or lack of knowledge about the true, divine model of supply and demand. The second is our willfulness.

We may know on some level that tithing works. Unless we become willing to put the principles to work in our lives, however, we won't experience the full force of the abundant flow of prosperity. Want to test the theorum of tithing for yourself? Want to see how you can put the prospering power of tithing to work in your life? First, you must learn how to give without attachment. Next, you have to learn how to give in gratitude and with thankfulness. Finally, you have to learn how to give thanks for what you already have in all areas of your life—even when what you have doesn't look anything like what you would have chosen.

When you give thanks for everything God has provided to you, the Universe responds by opening up even greater good to you in the form of rich ideas, gifts and abundance in all areas of your life.

We have to learn how to let go of our attachment to the outcome of events in our lives. The mantra of "I want what I want when I want it" needs to be replaced by a willingness to let things unfold in Divine Order. Let go of your *expectations* of "how" something should appear in your life and you make room for the *expectancy* that what appears will be for your highest good, even if you don't see how in the present moment.

The Natural Benefits of Tithing

God multiplies blessings back to us and brings us out of the
land of just enough and into the land of abundance.
— Rev. Bob Yandian

In 1940, a man named Perry Hayden set out to prove that tithing was part of the Divine Law of Prosperity. He planted one cubic inch of wheat, in a plot four feet by eight feet (just to give you some perspective, it takes 2,150 cubic inches to make a bushel). From that first planting, Perry harvested 50 cubic inches of wheat. He tithed ten percent to a local Quaker community and planted the remaining 45 cubic inches of wheat the next spring. By the third year, the amount of land required to plant the increase had grown from the original 48 square foot plot to one acre. By the fifth year, the amount of land required to plant the increase had grown to 230 acres and yielded 5,555 bushels of wheat.

Perry Hayden proved that every harvest is an increase or multiplication of the seeds we plant. Farmers can only plant a new crop if they set aside seed or money from the current crop to purchase the future seed. We can only do the same in our lives. Like the Biblical story of Jacob, we too can plant our seeds and reap our harvest in all areas of our lives.

Once you make a commitment to tithe the first fruits of your labor—the first ten percent of your income to your Spiritual Source—like Jacob, you will discover that the benefits of tithing include, but are not limited to, monetary abundance. Abundance doesn't come merely as a windfall of cash. When you put yourself firmly in the flow of the Divine Law of Prosperity by actively tithing, you will receive creative, inspired ideas; gifts of all kinds; wisdom and guidance; improved relationships; increased health; the best customers, clients, contracts, opportunities, deals and so much more.

Prosperity isn't just about money. Prosperity is also about having more joy, more vitality, more health, more freedom and peace of mind. Tithing helps you be in the right place at the right time; it puts you in alignment with your highest good and protects you from harm.

> An admitted packrat decided to tithe of his possessions. One month, he tithed possessions in addition to his monetary tithe, equal in value to 65% of his income; the next month, 67%. Each month he found he was able to pay off over $1,500 worth of debts. He had not been able to put that much toward his debt repayment in many months. In addition, he calculated the gifts he had received since he started tithing: he lost weight, and was told to pay a lower rent than he expected when he moved. Monetarily, he received unexpected gifts as well: $150, $500 and $50. He also credits tithing as the reason he was saved from losing $45,000.

> He had put a bid on a house he wanted to
> buy but the deal wouldn't go through. One delay
> after another occurred. Eventually, he had the
> wisdom to withdraw his offer. Afterwards, he
> discovered that the house he had bid $105,000 for
> had major foundation problems and wasn't worth
> more than $60,000. Had the sale gone through, he
> would have owned a house worth $45, 000 *less*
> than what he had paid for it.

Tithing may not necessarily bring you more money. It may just provide you with a more efficient and effective distribution system for the money you already have, which may be what you truly need. When famine swept Ethiopia in the 1980's, a massive global relief effort was undertaken and more than five hundred tons of grain were shipped to Ethiopia. Despite these efforts, very few hungry people were fed and the grain rotted in warehouses in the port cities. What Ethiopia truly needed was not more food but more trucks and better roads. The country had enough food. It merely needed a better distribution system, so the food they had could be used for the highest good of all. You may already have "enough" money. You just may not have the best system in place to allow you to use the money you have for the highest good of all, yourself included.

God doesn't hand over everything we desire in the form in which we desire it. God often gives us the tools that we require to succeed and then guides us to discover how to use them.

> Mary Hart, the long-running host of the
> "Entertainment Tonight" show is a firm believer
> in focusing on the positive and not the negative.

In 1979, she left journalism behind. She drove to
Los Angeles with $10,000 in the bank and dreams
of acting stardom. She wanted to have her own
show to be reported on; she didn't want to report
on the acting business.

She lived in Westwood and jogged through
the swank neighborhoods of Holmby Hills and
Beverly Hills, consciously saying to herself every
day, "Someday I will be successful enough to live
in this neighborhood." She visualized herself in
that community of success. Today, she and her
family live in one of those neighborhoods.

What Mary Hart ultimately learned was that she was in
the best place she could have been in. She once said "I knew
this job was good and I knew it was fun, being thrust into the
middle of all these situations that I dreamed about. But just in
a different way than I'd dreamed about."

When you practice the art of tithing, you will receive six
incredible benefits:

1. Increased wisdom and good judgment.

2. Increased health.

3. Increased wealth and a greater ability to meet expenses
and reduce debt (often through the reduction of those
expenses).

4. Increased fulfillment in relationships.

5. Increased spiritual understanding.

6. A willingness to let go of your expectations of what
you believe you desire—so you can become open and receptive
to receiving what you truly need.

When you begin to realize these benefits, you will be able
to give even greater good, above and beyond the first ten
percent.

Many other industrious and prosperous business leaders practiced tithing, including the Colgate, Kraft, Templeton and Heinz families. William Colgate learned about tithing from an old riverboat captain. Colgate ultimately tithed 50% of his annual income and his bookkeeping records were marked "Account With the Lord."

When people chastised John D. Rockefeller for having so much money, he was not dismayed or ashamed of his wealth. He simply stated one true fact to those who criticized him. He told them, "God gave me my money." Rockefeller started tithing in 1855. His income that year was $95 and he tithed $9.50 to his local church. Between 1855 and 1934, he gave away over $531 million, tithing far more than 10% of what he had been given.

In fact, some people who tithe eventually discover they can effortlessly give away 90% of their income and live comfortably on the remaining 10%. John D. Rockefeller experienced this joy, as did R. G. LeTourneau (the man who invented the heavy equipment that later became the foundation of the Caterpillar company) and Rev. Stretton Smith (creator of the 4-T Prosperity Program).

What did they know that we don't know? Their families taught them how to be good stewards of the abundance they had been given. They were taught—just as Biblical stories show that Abraham taught his son Isaac and Isaac taught his son Jacob—to give thanks for what they had been given, by giving back. You may have been taught tithing. You may have been taught the rightful purpose of tithing or that tithing was an obligation or a duty, if that is what your family believed.

Either way, having the knowledge about tithing is not what prospers you, any more than having the knowledge that the angles of a triangle always equal 180 degrees helps you be a better builder. You have to put your knowledge into action. These successful people learned how to tithe from their families, but it wasn't until they seized the opportunity to *practice* the art of tithing that they were prospered in all areas of their lives.

It is only through acts of impersonal, selfless giving that we are prospered. Tithes that are given willingly, cheerfully and joyfully are the only tithes that count. These are the true tithes, no matter how large or small they are. In a story found in the biblical book of Mark (12:41-44), Jesus watches as people give their tithes to the temple and he comments on a woman who willingly gave her last two copper coins to the temple, saying "I tell you the truth, this poor widow has put more into the treasury than all the others. They all gave out of their wealth; but she, out of her poverty, put in everything–all that she had to live on."

The joy with which we give is what empowers a tithe. Whatever you give, give it with praise and thanksgiving, not out of resignation, desperation or with annoyance. When you give your tithe, you must learn to give it, as you should with any gift, without attachment.

> A man who spiritually fed his congregation was going to begin his ministerial studies and many members of the congregation tithed to him for his lodging, his transportation and his tuition. When circumstances changed and he was unable to attend as planned, he tithed what he had been given to someone who fed his spirit whom he knew also wanted to enter the ministry. This caused some concern among the people who had

39

> tithed to him. Some people who had given to him
> were aghast that their gift had not been used as
> they had expected.
>
> To help ease their turmoil, I asked them,
> "Was the money a gift or a loan?" "A gift," they
> replied. I then asked, "When you give a gift, who
> does it then belong to?" "The person you gave it
> to," they replied. "Then it belongs to him, and
> what he does with it is none of your business."

When you judge yourself or others and find a shortfall of some sort, stop and acknowledge your judgment. If you find yourself judging a financial situation or choice someone is making, especially with a gift or tithe you give them, it is usually because you are being reminded of an event in your life where you felt judged by someone. Ask yourself: "Who in my life did I perceive as having judged what *I* did with *their* money?"

The following **Dollar a Day Exercise** will help you release your resentments and attachment to money you give. Take a dollar (or your currency of choice) every day, and give it away to the third person you meet each day. Tell them you wanted them to have this gift. Pay attention to both their reaction and your reaction. Write down everything that comes into your head about what you think they will do with the money and how you feel about it. Then ask yourself *why* you believe it matters what they do with *their money*? How does what they do with *their* money relate to you?

Remember the last time you gave someone a gift or did something nice for someone and didn't even receive so much as a "thank you" in return? That person's lack of gratitude made you think twice about going out of your way to give them more, didn't it? Have you ever bought a toy for a child? What usually happens? You give the child the gift and within ten minutes the toy is in pieces. Or you give the gift and never receive a "thank you", much less a thank you note. What thoughts run through your head at these times?

"Why did I spend my money on that?" "That's the last time I'm going to waste my money like that." These are the thoughts of lack that enter our heads whenever we give with an attachment. We have the misconception that somehow we lost money when we bought the gift, or that we lost respect or honor, because we believe our gift wasn't properly appreciated or valued.

Our attachments and expectations make us susceptible to the belief that somehow we can lose something we have in our lives. The Law of Energy has proven otherwise. Everything in the universe is made up of energy. And energy can be neither lost nor destroyed—it can only be converted.

Giving Thanks

Chapter Two: Tapping Into the Spiritual Flow

Jehovah-jireh: The mighty One whose presence and power provides,
regardless of any opposing circumstances.
— Charles Fillmore

You can tap into the spiritual flow in your life in two ways: as abundance comes into your life and as it goes out. As I said earlier, in its most literal sense, tithing is defined as giving away a tenth, usually ten percent of your income. In a broader sense, however, the art of tithing involves sharing a tenth of your time, talents and treasures— including your income—with people or organizations that feed your soul, as a way of giving thanks for the good that appears in your life and that is forthcoming. Wherever you receive spiritual inspiration, joy and help is where you should tithe.

Always tithe to places that spiritually feed you. Your local spiritual home and leaders are the best starting point, if that is where you receive your spiritual help. Some other places to tithe include musicians, children, waitresses, speakers, writers, sometimes friends or family members, spiritual organizations, ministers—anyone who provides inspiration and uplifts your spirit. Doing so places you directly in the flow of Universal Energy and Abundance and brings you even greater good than that which you send out.

A tenth is described as "a small percentage." Yet ten percent can seem like a lot of money, can't it? There were days when I first starting tithing and the bills were coming in and a due date was looming and the checkbook balance looked a little slim when I thought, *I don't know if I can afford to tithe this week.* When I examined my fear, I discovered I had a false belief that my tithe was coming from *my* money, and that there was a limit to how much money I would, or could, have.

You may struggle with the concept of tithing, because you think you are giving away 10% of what is *yours* instead of giving thanks for the 100% you have been given by passing along 10% as seed money for the future. This may be because you have an attachment to the 10%. True freedom comes from letting go of our attachments.

> A well-to-do woman, whose children attended the inner city school where she taught, opened her home readily to her children's poorer schoolmates even when she wasn't home. Her friends and co-workers expressed dismay, since any time they had done the same, items they owned went missing. This woman believed firmly that everything in her home was merely a possession and that if a child truly thought he or she needed it more, they would take it, regardless of whether she was there to stand guard. She knew she was the steward, not the owner, of these possessions and she trusted God, not the schoolchildren, to do what was right and fair with these items. She released her attachment to these items. As a result, nothing was ever taken from her home.

Scientists have proven that everything, everywhere, is made up of the same subatomic particles. There is nothing that is not part of this invisible substance. Everything and everyone is connected and part of the whole of the Universe. What name do you give this connected substance? God, Universal Energy,

Spirit? Call this substance Spirit and you will see that Spirit is within everything—within every visible form of good we can see, and in all the things we cannot see. There is nothing that is not made up of Spirit. There is nothing that does not belong to Spirit. Every idea we have was inspired, meaning it was in Spirit before it was made manifest. Everything we possess is on loan from Spirit, because everything we have is created from this inspirational energy.

An attachment is nothing more than an outward manifestation of our fears. When you look at your life through your fears, it is as if you are looking through a kaleidoscope. Everything in your life appears to be fractured, but when you dismantle the kaleidoscope the whole picture clearly appears and the illusion is revealed to be caused by nothing more than three mirrors and a few bits of broken glass.

Until you come to this awareness of the wholeness of the Universe—that you are the steward and not the owner of the abundance in your life—you will be afraid to give your full tithe. As you work to overcome this fear and release your attachment, start the habit of giving a set percentage regularly (even 1%) until you can cheerfully, willingly and joyfully give a full 10% tithe—or more!

The *only* time you should tithe is when you can do so cheerfully, willingly and joyfully. A woman came to me upon hearing that I would soon be speaking at her church. She said every week she thinks about tithing. Every week she gets out her checkbook and says, "Okay, this will be the week I will tithe." But every week a fear steps in her way, and she cannot do it. So she gives what she can give willingly, cheerfully and joyfully that day. And this is what I say to you: She will receive

45

a greater blessing for her partial tithe than the person who resentfully or fearfully writes a check for a full 10% and drops it in the offering basket. The person who views the tithe as an obligation and a duty will not prosper more than the person who gives all he or she feels capable of giving, but gives it with love.

The abundance you will receive when you willingly and cheerfully give a portion of your tithe is but a fraction of what is available to you once you can move beyond the fear of tithing a full 10%. Once you get out of your own way and allow God to take the reins, abundance will come galloping into your life.

Meeting Your Every Need

Prosperity depends less on our financial situation than on the extent to which our needs are being met.

— Shakti Gawain

Whatever percentage you give away to places that feed your spirit, always write your tithe check first. Do this for 30 days and you will soon see that the 90% you have left over after tithing throughout the month often goes as far, or farther, than the original 100%. Even if your income doesn't increase visibly, you'll still do as much or more with the remaining 90%. That is because tithing connects you to God's flow of Universal Energy and Abundance.

Imagine, if you will, a space heater. The space heater has a power cord which is plugged into a socket. The space heater is connected to the flow of energy. However, the space heater can't access the flow of energy simply by being plugged in. Something has to happen to open the pathway to the energy. You need to flip the switch. Like the space heater, you're always connected to Universal abundance. Flashes of inspiration come to those who plug into the Universe, but you need to flip the switch in order to access this flow of abundance and inspiration. That's what tithing does for you. Tithing is the switch.

What happens when you flip on the switch? Let's go back to our space heater for a second. Once the space heater accesses the flow of energy, you have an increase in heat flowing into the room. At the same time, you also have a decrease of cold in the room. It's a two-fold experience. Like the space heater, by tithing, you place yourself in the flow of abundance where you have an increase in the money on hand as well as a decrease in the expenses that occur.

> A woman began tithing and noticed that while no windfall of cash had dropped in her lap her expenses seemed to be going down. She closed on a house and even though she had locked in a certain rate, the rate went down, causing her to have lower monthly payments. In addition, her closing costs were overestimated by $500 and her car insurance dropped $20 a month. When she added up the savings, they totalled far more than she had tithed to date.

This is how the 90% left after tithing goes farther than the original 100%—even with no increase in your income. The Universal Energy automatically bestows blessings on you to meet your every need in response to your act of giving thanks.

47

> A friend and I once ordered a pizza. When
> we went to pick up the pizza, we were asked to
> wait a few minutes, so we wandered outside.
> When we came back, the pizza man said, "Ladies,
> your pizza will be on the house. We had to remake
> it." With no effort on our part, we received the
> gift of a free dinner with a hearty "thank you."

If you are eager to give, God will accept your gift on the basis of what you have to give, not on what you don't have. In other words, give what you can cheerfully give, but give in a systematic manner.

When you give systematically to the Universe, the Universe will see even more clearly that you are ready to reap a larger harvest. Remember those raspberries from the Introduction? Some years, I harvested raspberries for weeks after the growing season should have ended, simply because I got up every morning and harvested the raspberries. I took the action and the results followed.

> A church had stopped giving money to other
> organizations. Overall income had fallen off and
> the church had used up its savings to make ends
> meet and had fallen into debt.
> I immediately encouraged the Trustees to
> tithe, but they were fearful. How could the church
> make ends meet with the 90% left over after
> tithing when they were unable to make ends meet
> with 100% of the church's current income? I
> asked them to have faith and test the principle of
> tithing. Eventually, they agreed to step out in faith
> and tithe three percent of the income from just
> the Sunday services.
> Over the next six months, the church tithed
> $371. Amazing things happened during that time.

An internationally acclaimed speaker who normally charges $3,500 to speak called and asked if he could speak for free. Then someone was so moved by a Sunday service they put a $1,600 check in the offering basket—which was more than the usual sum of total offerings collected at a service. Within two years, the church was tithing a full 10 percent of its income from all sources, had paid off all outstanding debts and had over $25,000 in savings.

This is just a sampling of what happens when you start embracing your abundance by systematically giving thanks for your existing good. The person who plants few seeds will have a small crop; the one who plants many seeds will have a large crop. Give as you have decided, not with regret or out of a sense of duty. God is able to give you more than you need, so that you will always have all you need for yourself and more than enough for every good cause. Give generously and your kindness will last forever.

Giving generously brings us back to the idea of stewardship. When we release our attachment to the idea that the abundance in our lives comes from us and from our actions, then we will truly prosper. We are the stewards of the abundance in our lives. We are granted the gifts of abundance in our lives.

If someone handed you $1,000 with no strings attached, would you be willing to give them $100 back, if you had no obligation ever to repay the remaining $900? That's exactly what God does. Everything you have, every dollar you receive, every gift you're given, every talent you possess, every relationship you have is on loan to you. Everything is on loan and may come and go, but the only thing you're asked to pay for its presence in your life is 10% of what you were given in the first place. Not a bad deal.

Whenever you experience challenges in any area of your life the first and best action is to take 10% of the income you receive and give it to people and places that feed your spirit. I can't stress this enough. Many people don't understand how they can tithe when they're struggling to make ends meet.

Tithing is the act of giving thanks for what you've already been given. You have this incredible business partner (named Spirit, God, Universe, whatever you choose) who has all the inside knowledge, energy and talent you'll ever need. Your business partner is ready, willing and able to share all this knowledge, energy and talent with you. In return, your business partner asks for only 10% of whatever you receive from that knowledge, energy and talent.

Most business partners demand at least 50% for this kind of contribution. God demands *nothing* from you. God merely provides you with an opportunity to give a portion back of what you were given in the first place. If I offered to share with you everything I know about improving your life, asked you to pay me nothing, and told you that I would continue to share my knowledge if you passed along 10% of whatever increased income you earned from my knowledge, would it be worth it to pay 10%?

God, who supplies seed for the farmer and bread to eat, will also supply you with all the seed you need and will make it grow and produce a rich harvest from your generosity. As you begin to give thanks with your tithe, you demonstrate that you are ready for even greater good. Your business partner sees this expansion in your prosperity consciousness and reacts by pouring out even greater blessings.

Release past negativity, fear and attachment and step out in faith with God as your business partner. You've learned the lessons of negativity, fear and attachment well, but it's time to move on to the graduate school of life where you actively choose the positive in your life. Pull up a chair and sit yourself down firmly in life's prosperous flow.

Everyday, remind yourself that you deserve the best and you have the best. When you do this, you will become like a hyperactive person who takes time to sit still in a garden filled with hummingbird feeders. You will no longer see whispers of prosperity whizzing past you. You will see your prosperity manifest in all its glory.

The Divine Law of Prosperity states that *universal abundance is unlimited and you can tap into it any time, simply by opening up your mind to the possibility that more good exists for you.* Set a goal for yourself today to start giving a percentage of your income to the source of your spiritual strength this month. It can even be as little as one percent.

Stagnation is death. Circulation is life. Picture a swimming pool for a moment. You cannot keep a pool clean unless there is a way for the water to filter out and filter back in again and you actively remove the debris that appears. Our job is to keep the outlet and the inlet open—to receive and to give—and to take action to remove the debris. It is God's job to keep the stream of abundance flowing in and through us. The only way to turn a belief into action is to express it in an outer, tangible form. Tithing turns the belief that everything comes from God into an active force.

51

The True, Divine Model of Supply and Demand

*I have absolute faith that anything can come to one who
trusts in the unlimited help of the Universal Intelligence within,
so long as one works within the law and always
gives more to others than they expect
and does it cheerfully and courteously.*

– Walter Russell

We have two models in our lives: the scarcity model and
the limitless model. By letting go of the scarcity model of supply
and demand that says others must do without in order for us to
have more, and embracing the limitless model, we can tap into
the greater flow of abundance.

Everything in the Universe consists of energy; matter is
nothing more than rhythmic waves of light, waves of thought
and action patterned into what we call substance or matter.
Light is the foundation of the Universe and the secrets of
creation lie in the wave, which is merely the physical expression
of energy. Everything is part of this rhythmic flow of giving
and receiving, part of a limitless supply of abundance.

The true nature of the Law of Supply and Demand is
that there is no limit to any supply. Until we have a specific
demand, however, we never tap the proper supply. Noted
economists Henry Hazlitt, author of **Economics in One
Lesson** and Paul Zane Pilzer, author of **God Wants You To
Be Rich**, recognized the true spiritual nature of this law. As
they discovered, when we have a demand the supply appears.

Yet the supply that appears may not appear in the form we expect it to take.

If we hadn't had a greater demand for gasoline in the 1970's, there would have been no supply of fuel-efficient devices. As a result of these devices, the amount of gasoline we consume per vehicle is smaller now than it was 30 years ago. The amount of gasoline is not the same as the supply of gasoline. The *amount* of any resource is not the same as the *supply* of any resource. The amount of money you have on hand is not the same as the supply of money that is available to you.

> One night, a farmer's four mules got loose and all were killed. Night after night, the farmer prayed for "a few more mules." Every morning, he took action on any idea he had to get new mules. Every day, the answer was the same: No new mules. One day, he approached the owner of the general store about borrowing money so he could buy more mules. There was a store policy against lending money; instead, the owner agreed to let the farmer buy a tractor over time. All along, the farmer had been praying for more mules, when God had something bigger and better in store.

Always ask yourself: What is your true demand? What is it you truly want? The farmer kept asking for "a few more mules." The farmer's true demand, however, was not more mules; his true demand was to find a way to plant his crops. By consistently taking the next step toward obtaining his new mules, he was able to find a new supply of power for planting his crops. His *supply* of planting power had changed from four mules to one tractor, but the *amount* of planting power had

53

actually increased, because one tractor was far more powerful than four mules.

To firmly understand the true nature of the law of supply and demand, you must learn to trust God to provide for you. You must have faith in the Divine Law of Prosperity to provide what you hope for and desire, even when you can see no evidence that the law works or is at work in your life. You must have faith in the Divine Law of Prosperity the same way you have faith in the Law of Gravity, even though you can see no evidence of that law working in your life. Tithing is spiritual economics at work, the same way an apple falling from a tree is gravity at work. When you tap into the spiritual Source of the economy you will never again see any downturn in the economy, no matter what the statistics may claim.

In the biblical book of Mark (21:22), Jesus said, "If you believe, you will receive whatever you ask for in prayer." Every thought we have is a form of prayer. Our thoughts form our reality and thereby form whatever we have present in our lives. Is everything in your life a result of hard work or luck (good or bad)? What about everything you do not have?

Do you feel the absence of what you desire is due to some lack within you, a run of bad luck, or the devil running amuck in your life? Is everything *good* in your life a result of what *you* have done while everything you *lack* is a result of what *others* have done to you?

I ask you to consider the possibility that the *only* thing you really lack is trust. Have you ever primed a pump? If you have, then you know you can't simply walk up and start pumping away expecting water to flow out. It may flow out if the pump was recently primed, but if not, chances are nothing will come out. You need to *add* water if you want to *draw* water from the well. So, too, with tithing.

Benjamin Franklin said, "He that kills a breeding-sow, destroys all her offspring to the thousandth generation." When you don't give your tithe, you destroy all its offspring—all the divinely inspired ideas and abundance it contained.

Building a Foundation of Trust

Trust God, and use what you have on hand to prime the pump to create greater good. Don't take what you've got, use it up and hope to find another source somewhere else down the road. Don't kill your breeding-sow. Nurture it with lovingkindness and thanksgiving, having faith in the abundance that will spring forth from it.

In the biblical book of Hebrews (11:1), Paul said, "Faith is the substance of things hoped for, the evidence of things not seen." Faith is derived from the Latin *fidere*—to trust. To have faith means to trust in the promise, to have fidelity to the promise, to abide by the promise and to have a sincerity of your intentions.

Divine laws are laws that cannot fail. Understanding these laws requires you to have faith based on principle. I'm sure I frustrated many a math teacher with my endless questions, such as: "I know one plus one equals two, but *why?*" and "I know that the angles of a triangle always equal two right angles or 180 degrees, but *WHY?*"

Faith is the evidence of things not seen. Faith means knowing something works and putting it to work in our lives even when we don't know *why* it works. Many people know

55

with *absolute certainty* that tithing works, although they do not know precisely *why* it works. Tithing works because the laws of the Universal Spirit, the laws of God, are eternal, unchanging truths. One such truth is found in the Divine Law of Prosperity: *A lavish abundance already exists to meet your every desire. Ask for what you desire with the absolute certainty that it will be given to you.*

> A woman who regularly tithes sent me an e-mail asking me to pray with her for her rapid certification in a new field. She sent off the e-mail and a few moments later received word from her instructor that her certification had been approved. Although I hadn't yet read her e-mail, she had received an instantaneous manifestation. She had asked with complete faith that her request would be granted, because she believed in the prospering power of my prayers. My actual prayers had nothing to do with the manifestation, since I hadn't even read her email before what she believed in had come to fruition.

I urge you to continually rejoice and thank God that you *have* (not that you will have) the desires of your heart. You already have the desire. Remember: The desire is the hope or promise of the things that are unseen. Because you already have the desire, your good is already yours. Your good is merely in the realm of supply that is currently invisible to you. Through your tithes, you manifest that good in your life in a visible form.

If you win the lottery but never claim your prize, it does not make you less of a winner. It simply means that you did not claim your good. You did not take the action necessary to claim your abundance and make it manifest in your life. When you envy something that belongs to someone else and you use it for your own benefit without permission, it does not make you more prosperous. It simply means you have claimed someone else's good. It is not the item they have—their spouse, their house, their car, their income, their possessions—that you desire. What you desire is the *equivalent* of what your neighbor or your boss or your friend has, and you want to claim this equivalent for yourself. You want the love, the comfort and the joy that is represented by these things.

When you begin to understand the true nature of the law of supply and demand you will begin to realize there is an unseen but unlimited supply of good for everyone. This is another part of the Divine Law of Prosperity: *No one needs to have less in order for someone else to have more.*

Affirm your rightful claim to your supply of love, comfort and joy rather than claiming the supply that belongs to another and your supply will manifest in your life, according to the Divine Law of Prosperity, in Divine timing. Do not ask for success and then prepare for failure—prepare for the success.

> I once needed to pay a $1,400 bill, but did not have all the money on hand the day before the bill was due. Rather than prepare for failure by rehearsing how I would convince my creditor to take my partial payment, I prepared for success by rehearsing how I would write out the check for the entire amount, address and mail the envelope, and then call to let the creditor know that payment in full was on its way. Later that afternoon, I received a large book order that more than amply covered the amount due on the bill. I thanked God, wrote out my tithe check and let the creditor know that the check was in the mail.

You must strive to believe in what you desire. What happens if you test the theory of limitless supply in a water pump while not fully believing in it? You pour the water in and pump halfheartedly. Or you give up, affirming your "rightness" in the situation with statements such as "I knew it wouldn't work all along. What did you expect, with a pump this old?" All your efforts will have been in vain. The water level will drop back down into the pump, even if you were mere inches away from an outpouring of abundance the likes of which you have never seen.

If you trust and keep taking action in faith you will be rewarded. That first cup—which you willingly gave back to the Source to "prime the pump"—will come back to you multiplied, filling up and spilling over like an endless waterfall until every container you have is filled to overflowing. The abundance you receive will provide you with enough to meet your every need—a luxurious bath, a hot pot of soup, filled canteens—and enough to share and to spare.

Your faith in the principle, your trust, is the power that will draw your good to you. If you allow yourself to have faith and tithe without ceasing for one year, no matter what occurs, you will be more prosperous in all areas of your life. Rest assured, you will be given what you asked for, or you will be given the means to have or achieve what you have asked for, *or something better*.

A man tithed and set his intention for his family's debt to be reduced to zero, affirming that he was open and receptive to "this or something better." Within 30 days, his company agreed to pay 100% of his tuition (which included weekend room and board) to attend Wake Forest's Executive MBA program. The cost was more than his family's debts and the payback over their lifetime is ongoing, because his salary will continue to rise now that he has his MBA.

This man's demand was for the elimination of debt. The supply that he received was increased wisdom, which would result in increased income. Receiving—the act of taking or claiming your good—is as necessary to putting the law of supply and demand into action as giving with gratitude and thankfulness.

It has been said that the ultimate resource is people— skilled, spirited and hopeful people. When you want a promotion at work, you need to give forth an effort that shows you can do the job you want. The same is true for any increase in abundance in your life. You have to be a good steward of the abundance you have already received.

Are you happy with what you already have, and do you use it wisely? If not, the Universe acts on the premise that you won't be happy with more if you can't be happy with what you already have. Do you want a new car? How do you treat the car you currently have? Do you treat it with lovingkindness, giving thanks for the transportation it provides, tithing of your time and attention, keeping it clean and in good running condition? Or do you treat it like a pile of junk, with disparaging words and neglect, while affirming that if you had a better car you would take better care of it?

Tithing—giving thanks for what you currently have— starts in your minds. It starts with a change in attitude about everything and everyone that currently exists in your life. Giving thanks always begins as an inside job.

59

Giving Thanks

Chapter Three:
Is It Possible More Good Exists For You?

A true desire is not to have, *but to* be.
— Eric Butterworth

How much abundance can you visualize coming into your life—realistically—in the next year? How about in the next 30 days? Do you base your answer strictly on the amount you *know* may come into your life from your paycheck, clients, tax refunds, consumer rebates, inheritances and the like? Or do you base your answer on your faith in what you desire?

A single mother called and left me a breathless message two days after attending my prosperity seminar. She spoke so quickly, the message sounded like Alvin and the Chipmunks had called: *"Paula, I wanted to tell you about an AMAZING prosperity story that happened to me, and I REALLY want you to call me back so I can share this AMAZING PROSPERITY STORY with you!"*

It was nearly midnight, so instead of calling, I made a detour to my study. At every workshop, I teach people the truth about tithing and then I give everyone a blank postcard and ask them to write on it something they want to manifest in their lives during the next 30 days.

Some people write their desires for stronger relationships, physical healing, freedom from fear, increased prosperity in some form or another. This woman had written a single dollar figure on her postcard: $10,000. I went to bed that night fairly 'sizzling with zeal and anticipation,' eager to

hear this woman's amazing prosperity story.
When she had arrived home from work
Monday evening, she began opening her mail.
Enclosed in one letter was a completely unex-
pected check for $8,000. We laughed and said she
had another 18 days to manifest the additional
$2,000.

How was this manifestation of a completely unexpected
$8,000 possible? Because this woman had learned how to get
herself and her limited thinking out of the way so she could be
in the flow—the divine flow, that is. Once she put herself in
the prospering flow of abundance—tithing on every level of
her life, including her thoughts, words, actions and treasures—
she manifested nearly everything she desired within 48 hours
of setting her intention.

Can you visualize an additional $10,000 coming into your
life in the next 30 days? Can you, like this woman, hold the
possibility in your mind? Or do you immediately dismiss it as
impossible, simply because you can't *earn* that much money
from your job in a month?

Skeptics who tithe with the firm belief that tithing does
not work, are not tithing. They are merely giving money away
with the expectation of getting something in return. This is
not giving thanks. This is conditional giving. This is giving to
get. This is bargaining. If I give you 10% of my income, then
you must do x, y or z for me. It is the "what's in it for me"
mentality.

Tithing means giving thanks. Giving in good faith and
letting go of all expectations of the outcome of any events in
our lives. It means letting go of the illusion that we control our

level of prosperity and the amount of financial abundance in our lives. It also means letting go of the illusion that we *can't* have something, because we don't see *how* it is possible. That is like saying the angles of a triangle can't always add up to 180 degrees, because we can't see *why*.

What you want is your business. *How* it comes into your life, once you set the intention and give thanks for it and for the good that already exists in your life, is none of your business. Let me repeat that: *What you want is your business. How it comes to you is none of your business.*

We can't give 10% of our income away and somehow believe that everything will turn out the way we plan. The truth is, tithing often causes ripples and changes in your life that may seem like the exact opposite of what you think you want, need and desire. Rest assured, even when things don't turn out the way we plan, things *always* turn out for our highest good.

> When I first started tithing, I was working my way up the corporate ladder. Within months, I was given notice that I was to be laid off from my well-paying editorial job. I continued to tithe, even with the knowledge that my paychecks would soon disappear (because I knew that my paychecks were but one channel of my good, even though I had no idea when or where the next channel would appear). I then let go of the expectation of the compensation I was going to demand from my employer. I did not explode when the president of the company said he didn't want to pay me any severance pay. By staying centered, I continued to tithe, firm in the knowledge that the omnipresent abundance of the universe was manifesting in my life, despite

appearances. Instead of offering me severance
pay my employer asked me to do several consult-
ing jobs. I wound up receiving twice the amount
my ego would have asked for.

Is Your Glass Half Empty or Half Full?

My cup runneth over.
— The Bible, Book of Psalms (23:5)

I sometimes begin my prosperity workshops by holding
up a glass of water, where the water level is as equidistant from
the top of the glass as it is from the bottom. I then ask the age-
old question: How would you describe this glass of water?

Some audience members say the glass is half-full. Others
say it is half-empty. What is the truth?

The truth is: The glass is full to the point of overflowing.
The glass is half-full of water and half-full of air, and this air
spills out, up, over, and into the Universal flow. Like the glass,
which you in your limited thinking see as half-full or half-empty,
you are already full to the point of overflowing. Universal
abundance is unlimited and you can tap into it any time,
manifesting the abundance in your own life, simply by opening
up your mind to the *possibility* that more good exists for you.

Think outside the box. Look at everything that exists in
your life already and embrace it wholeheartedly. See the good
in every situation and know that even greater good is about to
manifest in your life. Then do your homework. Take action on
your goals and make it a priority to begin systematically giving,
no matter how small your tithe or how large your debts.

Never, ever, apologize for the size of your tithe. Never state words like "we only have…" or "It's just this small amount…" particularly when you're giving your full 10% tithe. When you give everything you have, when you let go of your attachment to your possessions and money and see yourself as the steward of the good in your life, you affirm that you rely on God as the source of all abundance in your life. This opens you up to receive abundance from a multitude of channels, both expected and unexpected.

Getting Started Tithing

I first stumbled across the principle of tithing quite by accident. The events that laid the foundation for my discovery of tithing began in the early 1980's while I was living in New York City. One rainy Saturday, I sought shelter in a dinky basement bookstore where I discovered what I thought was a "get-rich-quick book." The rain was letting up and I was in a hurry to get back to my apartment in-between downpours. I loved the title (*Prosperity Secrets of the Ages*), briefly glanced at the table of contents, and bought the book. Once I got home, I thumbed through the pages and discovered the book was filled with biblical references. At the time I was not very spiritually inclined, so I put the book down unread.

Every time I picked the book up over the years, I put it down again, unread. Over the course of 13 years I moved often, and even though I gave away many books during each move, this book stayed with me somehow.

One day, I was having a rough time at work and couldn't sleep so I went to the bookshelf at two in the morning, looking for something to put me to sleep. *Prosperity Secrets of the Ages* caught my eye and I remember thinking, "Aha! *That* will do the trick!" The next thing I knew the sun was coming up and I had read half the book, which discussed how a fascinating concept called tithing could improve your life forever. I was unhappy at work and in other areas of my life. I had recently ended a decade-long relationship and moved into my own home in an area where I knew only one other person. I decided I had nothing to lose by testing the principles in the book. That morning, on my commute to work, I began doing the affirmation work and that week I began tithing.

I jumped in with both feet, tithing a full 10% immediately. Tithing was so foreign to me that I initially gave away 10% of my income to various charities. At that point in my life, I wouldn't have known if something were feeding my spirit if it walked up and injected food right into my soul.

I didn't know exactly how tithing worked any more than I knew how triangles worked so that their angles always added up to 180 degrees. I just knew that the divine laws that govern these principles were always at work in our lives. I encourage you to test the principles in this book for yourself and see what changes occur in your life.

When you tithe, you are putting God first. You are working with the Divine Law of Prosperity, and you cannot fail. Don't allow anyone to argue you away from your commitment to create permanent, positive change in your life. Stand your ground. Tithing offers a systematic way to create true and lasting abundance in all areas of your life. If you want to put tithing to the test for yourself, make a covenant with yourself to tithe for the next 12 months.

Starting today, commit to tithing 10% of all your income—and of every increase that comes to you—to wherever you are spiritually fed for one year. Then sit down and inventory everything you have: all your assets, your possessions, the abundance that is in your life in the form of relationships, spiritual growth, health, peace of mind, and so on. Next, make a list of all you feel you lack and all the desires of your heart. Note that I said all you *feel* you lack. The truth is, you do not lack anything. You only fear lack, and in your fear, you repel your good. Starting today, you're about to change that forever.

Put your lists away in a safe place and implement your covenant, in complete faith that the Universe will provide for your every need, no matter what outer circumstances occur, and no matter how strongly your faith is tested during the year. Stay the course, no matter what.

I guarantee, one year from now, if you faithfully give 10% of all your income—and 10% of every increase that comes to you—with a sense of thanksgiving and gratitude, your abundance will grow and the desires of your heart will manifest for your highest good.

> I began tithing by rotating my tithe systematically each week among four different charities. I observed my thoughts and feelings about tithing, including resentments that came up when my tithe wasn't acknowledged.
>
> Gradually, as I learned more about tithing, I was drawn to tithe to spiritual places and ministers. I tithed to prosperity advisor Catherine

Ponder, and then began tithing to a Unitarian-Universalist church and a Unity church nearby in Annapolis, even though I'd never attended them.

Eventually, I began to see tithing as a way to give thanks, to give a "glad offering" to God, as a way of showing my gratitude for all the blessings in my life. I stopped seeing the money I was giving as an obligation or a charitable donation and started seeing it as a blessing—to me. The larger my tithe was, the more I knew I'd been blessed that week. Anytime the 10% I gave had increased, the 90% I had left was that much more. As my spirituality grew, I was guided to tithe where I was being spiritually fed, and I began giving my tithe to places that nourished my soul each week.

Where Should You Tithe?

> *'Bring to the storehouse a full tenth of what you earn*
> *so there will be food in my house.*
> *Test me in this,' says the Lord All Powerful.*
> *'I will open the windows of heaven for you and*
> *pour out all the blessings you need.'*
> — The Bible, Book of Malachi (3:10)

Every now and then, a new subscriber to my newsletter, *The Art of Abundance* (www.ArtOfAbundance.com), will write me and chastise me for perpetuating the notion that you can "give your tithe to anywhere you want." These well-meaning souls generally refer to the above scripture from the book of Malachi as evidence that all tithes are to be given to your local church.

68

Some aspects about tithing have been widely misunderstood by religious institutions, leaders and followers, which is partly why this book evolved. Some people believe we are obligated to give our tithes directly to religious organizations. Others believe we are not blessed by our tithes, but are only blessed by what we give above and beyond our tithes. It is true that you are not blessed by simply giving away 10% of your money, which may be where this belief began. You are blessed when your 10% is a *true tithe*, when you are using your tithe to give thanks for the abundance you have been given.

Where should you tithe? To the storehouse—those people and places that spread the word of God, of Spirit, of Allah, to those people and places who make you feel like you are in Spirit, those people who bring you inspiration. Bring your tithe to those people and places that minister to your spirit, regardless of their theological credentials. Where you worship may or may not be where you find spiritual inspiration. If you are spiritually fed where you worship each week, then that is *exactly* where you should be tithing. Your tithe allows the people who provide you with spiritual inspiration to feed themselves, which in turn allows them to continue to feed your spirit and the spirit of others whom they have not yet met and to send their tithe out into your local community. Your tithe guarantees that there is "food in my house," as the scripture says.

In Jewish temples, no collections are taken at services; each temple is self-supporting through the tithes of its members, with one exception: they charge a fee for admission to High Holy Day services. It is my hope that as we move beyond the obligatory tithe and reclaim the true giving nature of the tithe, one day even those services will be made available to all who desire to attend them, regardless of financial ability.

Many people have a strong negative emotional reaction to tithing, because we have largely strayed from the original meaning of tithing: to give thanks to God for the blessings we've received and to demonstrate that we are putting God first in our lives.

Tithing has gotten a bad rap. Some religious institutions try to calculate their annual budgets based on their members' projected contributions, instead of trusting God to supply them with what they desire. This is why they try to convince their congregations that the tithe is mandatory and offerings are optional. Unfortunately, this fear-based mentality (masquerading as "fiscal responsibility" or "sound money management") keeps the organization in a perpetual state of lack. If you want to raise greater funds for your organization, you must first raise the prosperity consciousness of your members. Help people see that they have an opportunity—not an obligation—to bring their tithes into the storehouse to receive God's blessings.

When you tithe, it may be appropriate to tell the person or organization why you're tithing to them, or you could send a note that says "thank you for feeding my spirit" or any other kind words that come to mind. On occasion, you may find it better to tithe anonymously.

A few years back I learned of a tragedy that had happened to a local family. Their tragedy reminded me of my good fortune. I tithed anonymously with a note telling the mother to use the money for something to feed her own spirit,

so she would have the strength and courage to be
there for her children (her husband/their father
was killed in a freak accident). Because we lived in
a very small town I was concerned the woman
might be embarrassed by the gift, so I sent it
anonymously. I didn't want pride to prevent her
from accepting the gift.

When you tithe, give your tithe with no concern as to
whether or not your tithe is "needed." It's easy to make the
snap decision that your tithe is not needed if the place where
you are spiritually fed reports that it has received an abundance
of tithes, or is needed because the place where you are spiritually
fed reports a great need. Do not allow yourself to be distracted
by fearful thinking that they do, or don't, need the money as
much as some other place might.

Always give to wherever you are spiritually fed, regardless
of perceived need. Give your tithe out of a sense of
thanksgiving, not out of a sense of charity. God works through
the people around us to feed us, and only God knows the true
need of each of his teachers and ministers.

I once was clearly guided to give my tithe
directly to my minister, rather than directly to the
church I attend. I was confused at first, but God
was very insistent that I should tithe directly to my
minister. I did not understand the reason at the
time. My minister later told me my tithe arrived
just as she was trying to figure out how to pay for
the plane ticket she'd ordered so she could travel
to Florida to be with her husband who was having
a health challenge. The amount of my tithe was
exactly the amount of the airline ticket.

I never again doubted where I should send my tithe. Since then I've always sent my tithe to where I was spiritually fed that week or that day.

The Mechanics of Tithing

What we give multiplies and circulates back to us
through the dynamic law of giving and receiving.
Not only the time, talent, dollars and love that we give,
but also the resentment, the smallness, the bitterness, will do the same.
— Mary Manin Morrissey

Tithing is about giving thanks for what you have already received and for what you anticipate you will receive. As I've said before, tithing is not about giving to get. However, the more fully you tithe, the more blessings wind up being bestowed upon you. This is God's promise to you. How much you actually tithe is up to you. What limit do you want to place on the opportunities in your life?

The ideal 10% tithe is from your gross income, but not everyone can comfortably embrace that idea from the start. Tithe on whichever—gross or net—you can cheerfully, willingly and joyfully tithe. I encourage you to start with 10% of your net income after taxes but before retirement plan contributions and the like.

A true tithe for a business owner would be 10% of gross profits. The tithe that would be due on net profits would be approximately 3% of gross profits. Every quarter, increase your tithe 1% of gross profits, until your company is tithing a full 10% from gross profits.

If you borrow money, tithe 10% of the money you borrow. Income is income no matter what form it takes or what channel it arrives from. If you live beyond your means and use credit to purchase goods and services, tithe 10% of the amount you "borrow" from creditors. Include the amount of credit you borrowed as if it were actual income you received, since you've already exchanged that credit for goods or services you desired.

If you're tithing from your net income, make sure you tithe from your tax refunds as well. This will eventually make it possible for you to tithe from your gross.

> A woman felt like she had created a financial imbalance after not tithing from her local tax refund and was afraid to spend her federal tax refund without taking care of her tithe first. She realized that she was operating out of fear, because she felt like she was out of the flow of prosperity in her life. She used the federal tax refund to pay both her tithes and immediately found relief from her anxiety.

When you tithe on your net income, your income tax refunds represent money you haven't paid a tithe on yet. Give thanks for the Universal stream of abundance God has prepared for you by tithing 10% from your tax refunds. Tithe as a way to say "Thank you, God" for your home, for all the blessings that have been bestowed upon you, for everything good that has come to you and all the growth opportunities that were revealed to you during the previous year.

Eventually, you will be able to tithe on the tax as well, and you will suddenly find you're tithing from your gross after all.

Remember this: The person who plants a little will have a small harvest, but the person who plants a lot will have a big harvest. Give as you have decided in your heart to give. Do not give when you are sad. Do not give because you feel forced to give. Do not give out of habit or out of a sense of obligation. God loves the "cheerful giver"—the person who gives happily. God can give you more blessings than you need. When you actively take part in giving your full 10% tithe, you will always have plenty of everything and enough to give to every good work.

What's Stopping You From Tithing?

However small your capabilities may seem at present to you,
you are just as much a necessity to God as the most brilliant intellect,
the most thoroughly cultured person in the world.
Remember this always, and act from the highest within you.
— H. Emilie Cady

Many people believe they simply cannot afford to tithe, based on the erroneous belief that their income is coming from them or from their hard work, and not from the Universe in the first place. A very real fear accompanies this, and if you find yourself in this situation, the exercise below will help you ease into giving thanks with your full tithe.

If you truly believe you cannot afford to tithe 10% of your income, try tithing everyday for just the next 21 days. Psychologists say that it takes 21 days to make something a habit. Tithe 10% of any income that you receive the previous day for 21 days to develop the habit of tithing, and to see how far your remaining 90% goes. After 21 days, if you still don't feel comfortable tithing a full 10%, drop back to a percentage you feel you can reasonably handle. As your income grows, so too will your tithe.

Only you can determine your comfort level. If you currently give set amounts to your place of worship or to charity, change your thinking about the amount you're giving and begin to tithe a percentage based on the dollar amount you're currently giving. If you routinely give $5 or $20 to wherever you are spiritually fed, for example, calculate what percentage of your weekly income that dollar amount represents and say to yourself: I am now tithing X%—3% or 5%—the percentage the dollar amount represents. This way, you will begin to consciously tithe that percentage from here on out. For example, if you bring home $1,000 every two weeks, and you routinely give $20 a week to your church, that $40 represents 4% of your income. From now on, commit to giving 4% of your income, from all channels, every week.

When you consistently give the same amount regardless of your income, you block your flow of abundance. Give a percentage of your income systematically, so you can see the greater abundance in your life. Track your abundance. Track your daily income and gifts. Each month, make it a goal to increase your tithing percentage by 1%. If you start tithing 3%, within seven months you'll be giving thanks with your full tithe.

Many people come to me and say they want to tithe but they are so in debt they can't even meet their current obligations. How in the world can they tithe if they can't even pay their bills? Believe it or not, the quickest way to get out of debt is to tithe your full 10% while you're in debt.

> A woman attended my *Break the Debt Cycle* workshop and set her intention to be debt free within a year. She created a *DebtBuster Strategy* that would have her completely out of debt within three years. She then implemented her plan and began systematically paying her tithes and paying off her debts. Thirteen months later, she was completely debt-free and even had a new car. If I had told her *how* her intention would come true, she says she would never have believed me.

Whether you're in debt to someone else or someone else is in debt to you, you can start tithing by giving thanks for the trust that created the original financial transaction. Write out your tithe check and give thanks for the limitless Source from which your current conditions came from. In this way, you begin to form the habit of blessing everything you already have.

> A woman applied for a loan to pay off her credit card debt [to reach her intended desire of being debt free], but the loan was declined. She had taken herself out of the flow of abundance and tried to take control of the reins herself, learning an important lesson in prosperity work: you can't get out of debt by borrowing money (borrowed money, of course, is still debt).

The Universe will give you abundant ideas on how to get yourself moving on your debt reduction if this is an area that needs work in your life. Hold the consciousness of what your life will look like when you're debt free. Then take action toward actively paying off the debt day by day, through the choices you make with the way you spend your money, while giving thanks by paying your tithe before you pay anything else. Your goal of being debt-free will manifest much quicker when you concentrate on prosperity and abundance principles than when you concentrate on chasing new sources of income. *Be still and know.* Knowledge of the next right and perfect financial step will be revealed to you in the stillness.

Many people contact me because they don't currently have a steady stream of income and they want to know how they are supposed to tithe 10% of nothing. Or they vow that they've made a commitment to tithing, which they'll start the minute they receive some income. The best way to create a new stream of income is to willingly give before you receive. Give on faith, like Jacob, that your blessings will be poured out for you.

Start tithing on whatever amount you have on hand. Tithe 10% of the cash in your home and 10% of the amount in your savings and investment accounts, especially if you've never tithed before. Tithe 10% of whatever is in your change jar. When you demonstrate your willingness to tithe on what you've already been given you open up untold doors to greater abundance.

Since we live in a consumer age, greater abundance usually leads us to greater spending. Which is why I get many questions from people who are having a challenge saving money while practicing the art of tithing. Financial experts direct us to "pay ourselves first" by setting aside 10% of the income we receive.

If you're paying your 10% tithe, and then setting aside 10% in savings, how on earth would you ever survive on 80% of your income? Acknowledge your fear, and then put in place a systematic way to build your savings while continuing your commitment to tithe. As your prosperity consciousness expands through the art of tithing, you'll find it's easier to make the leap to living on 80% of what you previously had lived on.

Until then, start gently. For one week, tithe 10% of your income to your spiritual source, and set aside 1% for your savings. The second week, tithe 10% and set aside 2% for your savings. The third week, tithe 10% and save 3% and so on. In ten weeks, you'll have increased your income and your savings to the point where you are effortlessly tithing your full tithe while setting aside a full 10% in your savings.

What "Can't Afford" and "Costs Too Much" Really Mean

The nature of gratitude helps dispel the idea that we do not have enough, that we will never have enough, and that we ourselves are not enough.
— Wayne Dyer

Your words are powerful, and you create your world by your thoughts and words, which is why it's important for you to know what you are really saying when you say, "I can't afford" something.

What you're really saying is, "I'm not worthy" and, "I'm not good enough." Your words reflect how you value yourself. What do you believe you can't afford to do? You believe you can't afford to do the things you want to do. What does that say about the importance you place on what you want?

"I can't afford to" is an excuse. You can afford to do anything you desire. Having what you desire, however, might take a little more effort than you're used to expending. A more accurate statement would be, "I'm not willing to pay the cost." Be honest with yourself. Are you willing to pay the cost? Or is the payoff of complaining about the current state of your life more appealing than the actuality of having what you want?

The same thing goes for, "That costs too much." When you truly desire something, nothing can keep you from finding a way to have it or create it. The next time you hear yourself say, "That costs too much", stop and analyze what you're really saying. What is it you're afraid to pursue for yourself? What price *are* you willing to pay for what you want? Do you want to pay off your debt and still go away on vacation? Then connect yourself with the divine flow by giving your full tithe and allow Spirit to bring your desire into manifestation.

Today's the day to start creating what you truly want. Start building the life of your dreams. The fact is, the only thing you cannot afford to do is to live your life with a mindset that supports you having less than the life of your dreams.

Giving Thanks

Chapter Four:
Becoming One With Life's Prosperous Flow

There should be no distasteful tasks in one's life.
Love anything you must do.
Do it not only cheerfully but lovingly and
the very best way you know how.
— Walter Russell

C reating the inner change that leads to your expanded prosperity consciousness may seem like a daunting task. So much of our world's abundance is currently trapped inside of fear and apathy. You may find some areas of your life distasteful.

Are there bills you haven't paid, because you're afraid once you do an emergency will come up for which you might need the money? Are you still in a relationship you've outgrown, because you're afraid you won't find anyone else who loves you or you're afraid of being alone? Are you clinging to old habit patterns that have outlived their usefulness, because you're afraid of the unknown changes that might occur if you give them up? Are you not pursuing a lifelong dream, because you are afraid of what changes might occur in your life? Do you go to work every day in a job that is meaningless to you, because you believe your job is merely a means of paying your bills? These may be a few of the fears that are holding you back.

Tithing gives you an opportunity to gently observe how fear may be holding you back from achieving your highest good. Just look. Observe. There's no need to actually make any changes right now. Just simply take the time to examine different areas of your life and recognize where you may be reacting out of fear, instead of actively embracing your abundance. This is the next step toward plopping yourself firmly in life's prosperous flow. Once you begin tithing, it's time to examine how you define abundance in your life.

How do you define abundance? What is it you truly desire? Are you looking for a specific dollar amount, or are you looking for what you truly want?

A woman asked me to affirm that a million dollars was now coming to her. I asked her what she wanted the million dollars for, and she said a home. Instead of affirming the million dollars, I asked her to walk me through what the property looked like and what the house looked like, inside and outside. I told her I would affirm the right and perfect home coming to her, as she desired.

A single mother of two small children was struggling with how she would ever find a home for the amount of the subsidized rent she was able to pay. I asked her to write down exactly what she wanted in a home, and let go of the fear that she would not be able to afford what she wanted. I asked her to have faith that what she desired would come to her. She called in amazement a few weeks later to delightedly share that the right and perfect house was now hers, at the rent she could afford.

When you find yourself in a situation that is distasteful to you, particularly a financial situation, it isn't the lack of money that makes you uncomfortable: it's your attachment to the money you do have. Maybe you're afraid of not getting "the right" value for your money, so you withhold your tithes or resent the fees others charge you. Maybe you're attached to seeing tangible proof of work, so you "give" money to someone like a musician in exchange for a concert or a CD, not just to say "thank you" when you hear their music.

Many people make this mistake with their tithes. They "give to get" instead of giving as a means of saying "thank you," because someone fed their spirit. When you give to get with your tithe, you're putting yourself first. When you give thanks with your tithe, you are putting God first in all areas of your life.

Practicing the art of tithing allows you to give up the emotional struggle that surrounds financial issues. Tithing teaches you how to release your attachments to the abundance in your life. When you release your attachment to the prosperity that flows in and out of your life, you allow that abundance to flow more freely.

Imagine that the flow of prosperity is like the water flow that comes through a garden hose. Having an attachment to the prosperity in your life is like putting a kink in the hose. When you release the kink in the hose, the water flows freely, just as the abundance in your life flows freely when you release your attachment to the flow. Your attachment is all in your mind, and it begins and ends with your thoughts and feelings about giving and receiving.

Tithing also allows you to sit quietly in the quicksand of your financial worries and observe your thoughts and feelings. When you begin to give thanks for everything that's occurring in your life, you begin to accept that your thoughts are either drawing greater good to you or repelling your good. When people share their good with you, it is because they are responding to the energy you have sent out that announces you are worthy and deserving of having good come to you.

Everyone and everything taps into this energy flow and willingly moves in ways that prosper you, in direct proportion to the way you willingly take action to prosper everyone and everything in your life. As this begins to happen, all you need to do is trust. Trust the Universe to provide you with everything you need, when you need it. Continue doing the work you do, because it is your mission to do so, not because it's the only means to make your mortgage or rent payment.

Consider the mission of Kamir Satish. He traveled completely around the world on a mission of peace in the 1980s. He carried no money with him on his journey. He trusted the Universe to provide him with food, shelter and safe passage across the oceans.

Even when surrounded by discomfort, he did not bemoan the job he had undertaken, or throw up his hands and quit in disgust. He quietly continued on his journey. He tithed of his time, his treasure and his talents, and the Universe responded by opening up untold channels of good for him to accomplish his desire to raise the global *peace* consciousness. Unwittingly, along the way, he also raised the global *prosperity* consciousness of every person he met.

You have it within you to do the same in your own way. Does anyone owe money to you? If so, I encourage you to practice the art of tithing as a way to clear up the outstanding debt that is owed you. Whenever you feel someone "owes you," financially or otherwise, you're stopping the flow of your prosperity. Resentments you hold onto for unpaid debts impede the flow of your good. Reaffirm the trust you placed in that person when you first extended credit to them. You believed, you trusted, in their ability to grow and prosper. Begin to see this person not as a deadbeat, unwilling or unable to repay you, but instead as someone who is growing more prosperous and giving every day.

Release the obstacle you've placed in front of the trust you originally placed in this person by writing a letter or making a simple phone call that says: "I've decided the money I gave you is a gift, and not a loan. Therefore, I now free you from any obligation to repay that money. I hope you will do the same for someone who owes you money." With all your heart, decide that this was indeed a gift.

Once you do this, amazing things will begin to happen. Years ago, I lent a friend $2,500. After I while, I realized I probably would never see the money again. So I wrote the above note, and released her from the debt. In return, I received a generous book order for several thousand dollars almost immediately.

By releasing my attachment to the form this abundance would take in my life, I made it possible for even greater good to come to me from elsewhere. Over the years, this same friend has tithed probably close to ten times that amount of her time and talents as her situation improved.

A Multitude of Blessings

Good, the more communicated, more abundant grows.

— John Milton

Most people think of their tithe as something they pay from their primary stream of income, such as their paycheck, and never give the practice of tithing another thought. Don't limit God to one income stream or you will forever be emotionally tied to the income from that channel. What if you get laid off, fired, or the company goes under? What if your best client stops buying goods or services from you?

As long as you think your abundance is limited to this one channel, you will forever be fearful of losing your income stream, until you open your mind to tithing from all channels of abundance in your life. When you become open to giving thanks and tithing from all the abundance that comes into your life, you will stay open to receiving abundance from all channels in your life. Tithe of your time, your talents and your treasures. When you tithe of your time, you often get back more time and the time of others. When you tithe of your talents, you get access to the talents of others. When you tithe of your treasures, you receive more abundance in all areas.

You may not always recognize the form abundance takes when what you are receiving is not actual dollars and cents. That's okay. The next step toward receiving greater abundance is to acknowledge your abundance in whatever form it takes, whether you're giving or receiving that abundance.

Start by looking at the many ways people have tithed to you recently, other than directly giving you money, and how you have tithed to others without directly giving them money. Then consciously look to see how you can tithe to others in the future.

A woman once shared with me a technique that reminds her of her abundance. She uses a little notebook to keep track of the income, expenses and gifts she receives every day. If someone buys her lunch, she records the dollar amount of the lunch as a gift. If she finds a dime on the sidewalk, she records the ten cents as a gift. If someone offers to carpool with her and she doesn't have to drive that day, she records the money saved in gas and automobile wear and tear as a gift. If she's out shopping and the item she intended to buy is on sale, she records the difference between the regular price and the sales price as a gift. Whenever she receives a hug, she records how much the hug meant to her as a gift. She carefully records a monetary value for each gift, so she can clearly see her abundance.

One day when I was out and about I decided to try this gift-recording technique. The results were astonishing. First, I dropped off a prescription at the pharmacy and got free lollipops. Value: 25-cents. Then I went to lunch and offered prosperity-oriented marketing advice to the restaurant owner, and I received a free $15 lunch and two free loaves of bread ($7). Back at the pharmacy, the expensive prescription was able to be filled with generic medicine—a gift of $70. At the grocery store two of the items on my list were

"buy one, get one free," so I received $6 worth
of free groceries. And last, but not least, I got
perhaps the oddest gift of all: a free pap smear.

As I have said, we don't always recognize the form our
abundance takes! My total gifts for the day were $208.25—not
a penny of which came in the form of legal tender.

What abundant gifts have you received in your life today
or during the past week that you have been overlooking? One
man tithed an article to my newsletter, plus some incredibly
valuable connections of people and organizations that came to
mind when he was reading about my work. A friend once tithed
a blue blazer to me, among other wonderful gifts. Friends have
tithed their homes to me for silent writing retreats. Others have
tithed their time and their talents, helping me get out seminar
mailings, making me meals, watching my dog, bringing me
breakfast, driving me around town, buying groceries,
proofreading, chauffering me to and from airports and speaking
engagements, offering legal or financial advice, sending me
inspirational articles, providing technical support, giving me
massages or making me laugh.

Start keeping a gift record, and see the abundance in your
life that is being overlooked. You can start right here, reading
this book. Count as a gift the uplifting spiritual messages you
receive as you read along. In addition, start keeping track of all
the ways you tithe to others. When you tithe, whether it's of
your time, talent or treasures, don't second guess *why* you're
doing something. Just make sure you're tithing to a place or
person who feeds you spiritually.

Freeing Up Your Trapped Prosperity

The only thing that stands between a man and what he wants from life is often merely the will to try it and the faith to believe it is possible.
— Ralph Marston

Always listen to your intuition—your inner voice—and tithe of your time, talent and treasures accordingly. Don't tithe where you think you *should* tithe, or try and rationalize whether or not you are tithing in the right place. Let Spirit guide you to spontaneously give your tithes wherever you are spiritually fed.

A church found its expenses were exceeding their income, and their savings were being depleted, even though the church continued to give away 10% of all its income. I soon discovered what was obstructing their Divine flow. They were tithing routinely without much thought as to where their tithes went. They had created a "tithing schedule" and were sticking to their schedule, rather than giving thanks to places that fed their spirit that week. They had begun to tithe to certain organizations out of a sense of obligation and not where they were necessarily being spiritually inspired. A few minor adjustments were all it took to get them back on track, building the church home of their dreams.

Are you tithing out of obligation, duty, or habit, or are you tithing where you are spiritually helped, inspired and fed today?

Many people give money to spiritual organizations and various charities for years and see no positive prosperous results in their lives. They tithe with the underlying sense that somehow they are bribing God to bring them money. They are in essence giving to get. This is a common tithing trap into which people fall. Your tithe is not intended as a bribe to God. Your tithe is a gift, freely given back to the Source where all your good came from, as a way of giving thanks for the gifts God has already given you.

Another common trap is tithing to a religious institution where you no longer attend or where you aren't spiritually fed. Are you tithing from habit, instead of from joy? Are you tithing there because you don't know where else to tithe, or because you believe you are supposed to tithe to your place of worship? Are you tithing there because you made a commitment to tithe through a stewardship program? Are you tithing, even unconsciously, in order to look good or prosperous in the eyes of other congregants or to get accolades for being a consistent donor?

I once had a minister comment that she was grateful I was conducting a prosperity in-service for her board members, because it appeared that some of them weren't tithing to the church on a regular basis. Imagine her surprise when I told her that *where* her board members tithed was none of her business!

When you practice the art of tithing, be sure you're tithing to your spiritual Source. One way to get into the habit of tithing to your spiritual Source is to spend 30 days tithing on the spot to anyone who feeds you spiritual food that day. Don't save your tithe up for the Sabbath; God's universal energy does not dwell only in a place of worship any more than it dwells in any other specific place. God is present everywhere, always.

What you need and want in order to do the things you desire and deserve doesn't come from your paycheck or your clients or your investment income. As scary as the thought may be, your financial prosperity may not come tomorrow from the same people, places and things where it has come from in the past. It may, and probably will, come in a different form than you've ever seen before. But your abundance will come, and it will come when you need it, if you release the fear that what you need and want won't be there and you step forward in faith.

There is One Source for your security. Whatever you wish to call that Source—God, Infinite Intelligence, Light, Love, Universal Spirit—is up to you. Whatever name you give your spiritual Source, don't withhold your good from the channels that connect you to that spiritual source. Give your tithe joyously, give your tithe gladly, and it will come back to you tenfold, hundredfold, even thousandfold.

Letting Go of Your Guilt Gifts

It is *the thought that counts.*
— Anonymous

Giving and receiving are part of the same cyclical flow of energy. You cannot be a cheerful, joyful, loving, willing, grateful giver until you learn how to be a cheerful, joyful, loving, willing,

91

grateful receiver, and vice versa. Yes, there may always be gifts that you're given that aren't something you need or want. Begin to see yourself as the steward of these gifts. Begin to realize that you are here to receive the gifts gratefully and to keep them in the storehouse until it is time for you to give them away.

My mother and I have vastly different tastes in clothes. My mom and her husband fulfilled a lifetime goal: traveling around Alaska for six months. For my birthday that year, she sent me a card with a beautiful note and a bright yellow t-shirt emblazoned with two polar bears and the word *Alaska* across the bottom. My sister Rebecca, with whom I graciously share my birthday month, received a similar t-shirt; hers was deep blue with two doe-eyed seals.

My mom and sister caught up with each other by phone one day, and Rebecca apparently didn't exhibit the "right" amount of enthusiasm for the gift. My mom wasn't offended (she's evolved into the knowledge that her tastes differ from that of her children!); she simply told Rebecca she'd replace the t-shirt with another gift, and she'd keep the t-shirt for herself. But then mom's gears started churning. If Rebecca didn't like her shirt, what about Paula? She immediately popped a letter in the mail making me the same offer.

The day my gift arrived, I immediately called and left my mom a thank you message on her answering machine. The loving words she had written in her card were worth thousands of dollars to me. Never mind that I rarely wear t-shirts or that bright yellow is not my best color. I

was touched by her thoughtfulness and that she
took the time to send a birthday present while she
was on vacation.

The very next day, a friend came to my home
and admired the t-shirt hanging off the closet
door. I asked her if she liked it. She said "Yes." I
said "It's yours." And the gift I received became
the gift I gave away.

My mom's letter asking if I liked the t-shirt
arrived a few weeks later, telling me to leave her a
message if I wanted a different gift. I didn't
respond, because I didn't want a different gift. I
appreciated the gift, even though it wasn't something I chose to keep.

Not too many years ago, I would have kept that t-shirt,
switching it dutifully from my dresser to my summer storage
and back again, moving it from one house to another. I would
have cluttered up my life with it, waiting with baited breath
every time I saw my mother for the inevitable question: "Where's
the t-shirt I bought you?"

So many times, we act, or don't act, because we're afraid
of offending others. We tithe, or don't tithe, because we are
concerned what others may think. We keep things we don't
want, or get rid of things we do want, because we don't want to
cause hurt feelings.

How many things in your home are taking up valuable
space and time, because you don't want to hurt someone dear
to you? It may be hand-me-down furniture from your parents,
kitchen gadgets from your sister, a tacky vase from an aunt,
crocheted coasters from your grandmother, a hideous piece of
artwork from your boss or co-worker. It may be something

you truly desired at one time, but which has now fulfilled its purpose.

What are you holding on to out of guilt? Why are you willing to offend your own sensibilities and encroach on your own space, but you're not willing to risk offending someone else? It's time to stop feeling guilty about embracing the things that resonate with your heart and let go of the things that don't.

You can never truly practice the art of tithing if you're not being honest with yourself in all your affairs. This is most especially true when you are receiving gifts from others. When you clutter up your life with the things you don't truly desire, you leave no room for your true desires to manifest.

There are three easy steps you can take with gifts to keep yourself in the flow of abundance. First, give thanks for the *intention* of the gift. Assume that the gift was given with lovingkindness and without strings of any kind. Other people may have personal reasons for giving you something, and those may appear to be strings that are attached, but in reality we're projecting those strings because we're not allowing the person to give their gift freely. We may be so wrapped up in not offending someone that we may perceive they are attached to the gift they gave when in reality, like my mother, they're only attached to our happiness.

Second, determine *why* you're holding on to a gift that makes you feel uncomfortable or that you don't like. Examine your motivation thoroughly. Why are you putting someone else's approval of you above your own comfort?

Third, find someone who will appreciate the gift more than you will. Then give them the gift.

94

An old friend had this down to a science. I remember visiting her home in New Jersey at Christmas-time, before she moved west. She would methodically go through the gifts she had received, showing them off one by one and relating a story about the person who had given it to her. Some gifts she would ask if I liked. If I answered affirmatively, she said, "Here, it's yours."

It was clear she held the gift giver in the highest regard and appreciated their love and the thoughtfulness of their gift. It was also clear that she realized she didn't have to hang on to gifts she would not use. There was no need to feel guilty about passing them along. She was thankful to have received the gift, expressed that thanks and then thankfully tithed them to me.

Practicing the Art of Unconditional Releasing

Your lasting good will never come through forcing personal will.
— Florence Scovel Shinn

You can practice the art of unconditional releasing whenever you tithe, whether you're releasing money, possessions, thoughts or the outcome of an event. One year, I was putting together birthday presents for a young niece and I was struck by the desire to give her a ceramic beaded figurine her great-grandmother had made for me. I knew in a few years this figurine would have great meaning for her and willingly released it to her.

Jump start the process of getting into the flow of abundance in your life. Look around your house every day for the next 30 days. Find one thing every day that you were given or purchased that you would like to release. Then give thanks for the item, release it, give it a new home (even if that new home is the local landfill), and sit back and watch what happens. Watch the change in the flow of abundance in your life. If clutter and debt are both challenges for you, I encourage you to read my book **Effortless Freedom From Clutter and Debt**.

Every time I systematically give away my treasures, I receive incredible gifts in return. Once, I gave away a whole batch of items I no longer desired to keep and I was immediately rewarded with new prized treasures including a 28" x 22" framed photograph of the beach, a wooden easel, three new sweaters and a new lamp. Throughout the month, keep a journal to record what you receive as a result of giving freely from your possessions as well as from your time and your talents.

Chapter Five: Practicing Acts of Courage

Courage is resistance to fear, mastery of fear—not absence of fear.
— Mark Twain

Why is it so hard to practice acts of courage with our money? Because the fear of not having enough has become an ingrained habit. My friend Barbara works harder than anyone else I know to break this habit. She once went into a restaurant to order dinner. A well-dressed man in the restaurant looked sort of lost, and her first thought was that maybe he was homeless but his clothes made her think otherwise. She struggled internally with offering him some food. Eventually, she walked over and asked him if he would like something to eat. His face lit up with gratitude, and he accepted her offer. So she bought two meals, one for each of them, and gave him dinner. But she did more than that, in truth. She fed his soul. The gratitude in his face fed her soul in return and was something she carried with her for weeks.

I've often struggled with my own intuition, as you probably have also, which says "give that person some money" when they ask (or even when they don't). Then the internal tape recorder clicks on, telling us they'll only use the money for drugs or booze or that the amount of money we have is all we have, and if we give it away then we can't get the chai latte we've been dreaming about all day.

Maybe you have an impulse to give someone a large amount of money—maybe your tithe that week is larger than usual, or you are moved to tithe more than 10%—but then you worry about how your gift will be perceived. Will it be viewed as charity? Will they think there are strings attached? Then our questioning mind goes into full swing: *Are* there strings attached? *Why* do I want to give this money? Should I give it all here, or divide it up into smaller amounts? What if I need this money down the road, if the car breaks down or a client cancels, or I lose my job?

Before you know it, you've talked yourself out of the courageous act of tithing that would have brought you closer to your own innate abundance. The only question you truly need to ask yourself is: What would Love do now?

We would all like to practice more generosity and less stinginess. But fear gets in the way. We fear not having enough. We fear needing later what we have now and we fear that when "later" comes we will not have what we need, or that others will not provide. We lack the faith we need to step out of our fear.

I once had the perfect opportunity to practice stepping out of my fear when I stopped to pump gas one winter day. I had a ten dollar bill and a hundred dollar bill in my wallet. I knew the gas attendant couldn't break a hundred, so my intention was to pump $10 worth of gas. As I went inside to prepay, I noticed a bedraggled man standing peacefully in the cold outside the gas station. I instantly thought I should tithe to him, but I realized the only thing I had available to tithe was a hundred dollar bill. *My* hundred dollar bill. Tithing a hundred dollars to a complete stranger seemed insane and I pushed the thought from my head.

I went inside and waited in line to prepay for
my gas and the thought came into my head again.
I went outside to pump the gas and saw him
standing there still, and the thought came to me
again. I had a complete conversation in my head
about the pros and cons of giving this stranger
my hundred dollars as I pumped my gas. What if
I need this money? What if there was something
else I was supposed to do with this money?

I walked past the man again to get my receipt
and immediately knew that God would provide
me with enough and more than enough, if I were
willing to give all that I had. So I decided right
then to give the man the $100. I walked outside
with my receipt in hand, reaching for my wallet,
and discovered that the man had disappeared. I
looked up and down the street and all around the
gas station, but he was gone. All God had asked
of me was to be willing to give; to have the
courage to believe that my abundance wasn't tied
to or limited to that hundred dollar bill.

Our fear is a tricky monkey. It tries to convince us that
everything will be okay as long as we have what we have. As
long as things don't change.

The truth is: Nothing is going to remain the same simply
because we want it to. Not our jobs, not our relationships, not
our finances, nothing. When things start to change, though,
our first impulse is to resist the change, usually with some sort
of aggressive feeling, thought, word or action. We rebel against
change and wrap ourselves around that rebellion, until it
becomes enmeshed in our lives. Until it *becomes* our lives.

The Venerable Buddhist nun Khandro Rinpoche uses a
wonderful example that illustrates how our resistance to change

keeps us stuck where we are, struggling against lack and limitation.

She likens life to a pillar with one end of a chain loosely wrapped around it. The other end is not tied to anything. Yet we pick up the end of the chain that looks loose, grasp it tightly and then blame the pillar for us being stuck where we are. We never look to see that we're the ones keeping us chained to an undesirable situation.

The only way to move past thoughts of lack and limitation is to embrace the willingness to let go. You must learn to cultivate courage, to cultivate the knowledge and the faith that abundance will flow in all areas of your life if you are open and receptive to it coming from many different channels.

Cultivating courage is not about fearlessness. Cultivating courage is about having a willingness to stay present even in the face of fear, even in the face of perceived loss. To not run from the hard, scary places in ourselves and in our relationships with others, or in our relationship with money. To not shut down or turn away in frustration, anger or disappointment, but to simply stay the course when your first instinct is to flee.

Courage is not about taking a defiant stance or stubbornly pushing your will through, no matter what. Courage is not about demanding that a situation go your way. Cultivating courage is about learning to be—to just be—with whatever is going on at that moment in your life.

Embracing Impermanence

A Chinese proverb says that water can either float a ship or sink it.
But did you ever notice that it's not the water
outside the ship that causes it to sink?
— Juanita Ruth One

True abundance comes when you stop grasping at the job or partner or income or other thing "outside yourself" as your source of prosperity. True abundance comes when you stop looking at yourself as being in pain and stop looking at something outside yourself as the thing that is causing the pain or as the only thing that can remove the pain.

Pain comes from a judgment you have made about something. Pain comes from a thought or feeling you had about a situation that occurred. When you become willing to let go of the judgment, when you become willing to change your viewpoint and your belief about the situation, the pain will disappear.

You must learn to be more comfortable with impermanence in your life. Impermanence frightens us because we are all control freaks at some core level, and we are all living in a world that cannot be controlled. The good news is there are three areas where you, and you alone, have complete control in your life: Your thoughts, words and actions. You create your life with every thought, word and deed. You, and you alone, can control your thoughts, words and actions. As long as your thoughts, words and deeds come from mistrust, you will not trust the good that appears in your life. You must take on the responsibility for relearning how to trust.

The biblical book of Jeremiah (17:7-8) says, "The person who trusts in the Lord will be blessed. The Lord will show him that he can be trusted. He will be strong, like a tree planted near water that sends its roots by a stream. It is not afraid when the days are hot; its leaves are always green. It does not worry in a year when no rain comes; it always produces fruit."

We all seek the balm that will help us alleviate fear so we can be more comfortable with the impermanence in our relationships, in our finances and in other areas of our lives. There is no balm. We cannot (and should not) alleviate the fear. That would be like treating the symptoms instead of treating the cause of the dis-ease (discomfort).

Instead, you must cultivate courage so you can dis-empower the fear. You must face the fear head on. In the movie *The Edge*, Anthony Hopkins and Alec Baldwin are stranded in Alaska with a man-eating Kodiak bear on their trail. The bear represents their fear. They can't outrun it; they can't hide from it. Fear feeds and relies on your running and hiding. You feed your fear when you allow yourself to be governed by the voices that say giving back a tenth of what you have been given will leave you with "not enough."

It is only by facing your fear head-on that you can catch it off guard. Once you catch your fear off guard, it is immediately diminished. It's disempowered and can be conquered. Practicing the art of tithing is the most effective way to face your fear head-on. Each time you tithe, your fear rises up—giving you an opportunity to recognize it and face it and disempower it.

When you tithe, and a money worry or fear comes to mind, remind yourself that you have three choices.

1. You can stay with the suffering and feed the fear. You can let the fear eat you up by withholding your tithe, or by giving your tithe while simultaneously holding onto the fear that by tithing you are giving away something you need, making a mistake or causing yourself to "not have enough" later.

2. You can do something that causes the fear to be masked, so you don't experience it now. This is a popular way of running away from the fear. You can repeat affirmations or deny the fear, trying to convince yourself that the fear is not real or warranted.

3. You can stay present, acknowledge the strength of the fear, face it head on and allow it to be converted into an impetus for action. You do this by looking at the good in your life. By recognizing all the ways—large and small—that your giving has resulted in you receiving even greater good in other areas of your life. Allow your fear to feed your courage. Allow your fear to feed your soul.

The best way to measure how in touch you are with your inherent, prosperous self is to ask yourself how well are you able to practice non-grasping? How well are you able to let go and take action, facing your fear head on? Giving thanks feeds your soul as much as it feeds the soul of those who receive your gifts.

When you become worried about the current state of your finances, health, relationships or other areas of your life, ask the Universe for simple reminders that your systematic giving has placed you in the Divine Flow. Even little, everyday reminders can help you stay focused on the prosperity in your life. Ask God to send you a simple reminder of your innate abundance every day, but especially anytime you start to feel your chest tighten over an issue. This will allow you to befriend the fear.

The signs may be as simple as a penny on the sidewalk or a note or gift from someone who expresses their thanks for you being in their life or for doing the work you do. Be receptive to these constant little reminders that you have everything you need today. Sometimes, all we need is a reminder that our futures are as bright as a newly minted penny.

Projecting an Aura of Abundance

Every man can multiply his own ability by almost constant wordless realization of his unity with his Source.
— Walter Russell

There's an old adage from the Twelve Step Programs that says "Act as If." Act as if you've got money, and money will come to you. Act as if you are confident in your abilities, and you will be able to achieve countless things. Act as if you are unafraid in a relationship, and you will find the courage to take the next step in that relationship. Act as if you understand how to handle money, and you will discover the information you need to be more comfortable about handling your finances. Act as if your health is improving every day and you will begin to feel more vibrant and energetic. Act as if you believe you have enough money to share and enough to spare and you always will.

> A man's jaw literally dropped when he learned a certain woman had grown up in modest circumstances. He was surprised to hear this because she actually exudes affluence. Everything about her, including the way she carries herself and her self-confidence, made him feel certain she had grown up wealthy. She attributed this perception as a direct result of her prosperity work and growing prosperity consciousness.

The words we speak, the clothes we wear, and the sturdiness of our posture all reflect our thoughts about ourselves and our abundance.

Do you whine about how hard your luck has been recently, how bad you are feeling these days, how awful your relationship is, how poor the economy is? Or do you point out how you feel something big is just around the corner, how you're feeling more healthy than the day before, how sweet your spouse was in some way, how business is looking up these days, how your income is growing every day, in every way?

Do you wear rag-tag, sloppy clothes, or do you crisply iron even your most threadbare t-shirt so you present an image of someone who cares about the life you've created for yourself so far? Do you slouch when you stand, giving the impression of someone who is beaten and victimized, or do you stand tall, expectant and grateful? Do you engage in sarcasm and gossip and encourage others to be righteously indignant or do you speak kind words, point out someone's good qualities and encourage people to work out their differences? Changing your inner and outer appearances are small changes you can make in your everyday life to tip the scales toward abundance.

While on a business trip to Chicago, I once had the good fortune of meeting a highly-motivated young woman named Cathleen Carr. With a little downtime on my hands I was looking for something to read, and Cathleen reached into her bag and presented me with a dog-eared copy of **The Tipping Point**, by Malcolm Gladwell. Although she'd long ago finished the book she carried it around with her for inspiration. After reading it from cover to cover in less than 48 hours, I could see why.

Gladwell believed that little changes could make a huge difference in our world. He looked at how epidemics (anything that has gained momentum and created exponential growth) have been tipped, or reached critical mass, simply by tinkering with the smallest details of the immediate environment. For instance, let's look at what caused New York City's murder rate to plummet in the mid-1990s.

It all started when New York City's new transit authority director shared his belief that the best way to create fundamental changes in people's beliefs and behavior on the subway system— changes that would persist and serve as examples to others— was to create a community where those new beliefs could be practiced, expressed and nurtured.

Following this theory, he began cracking down on the area where subway riders were being visually assaulted: subway graffiti. It became transit policy that no subway car would leave the train yard with graffiti. Next, he began targeting fare-beaters, assuming that the more often people saw others jumping turnstiles, the more often they would decide they shouldn't have to pay either. By catching and chaining gangs of fare beaters to the turnstile gates, his subway officers sent the message that lawlessness would not be allowed. No major changes were made in the way New York City police officers carried out their other duties or how they pursued other crimes.

Even so, violent crime, as well as petty crime, plummeted and continues to be lower than crime in many other cities. The tipping point for reducing the murder rate and increasing law and order in New York City resulted from eliminating everyday signs of disorder in the subway system like broken windows, graffiti and fare-beating.

What are the broken windows, graffiti and other signs of disorder in your life that invite poverty, lack and limitation into your life? Can the tipping point for reducing your difficulties and increasing your earning power, your satisfaction in relationships, your level of health and your abundance in all other areas be as simple and as trivial as repairing broken windows, eliminating graffiti and cracking down on fare-beaters? Can the tipping point for creating global prosperity be just as simple? After careful reflection, I decided it may be true.

Where are your broken windows? Where is your view distorted by old beliefs? Where are you acting as if you're impoverished instead of embracing the abundance that exists in your relationships, your financial affairs, your health and every other area of your life? Some of the most beautiful windows in the world are made of broken glass: stained-glass windows.

Where are you seeing or adding to the graffiti in your life? Graffiti can be verbal as well as visual. Your words carry immense power. Your words can tear someone down or build someone up. Your words can defeat you or your words can empower you.

You can eliminate the graffiti in your life by refusing to engage in gossip, refusing to take part in negative conversations about people and events and by consciously choosing to affirm the abundance in all things. Make a declaration of your independence from the economy. Declare that talk about recession, inflation, lack, poverty and debt have no power over you, any more than King George had power over the American colonists.

Where are you engaging in fare-beating? Where are you trying to get something for nothing? Where are you trying to beat the system, not being honest in your interactions with yourself or others? Are you surreptitiously taking time away from your employer or not working at your fullest potential, padding a bill to a customer, or withholding information from loved ones in order to avoid their hurt, disappointment or anger? Or maybe you're complaining about never getting a break while at the same time never giving others a break, or never giving thanks for what you already have, by giving a portion of it back to the Source where it came from?

By making a few simple changes in your outer circumstances, you can more easily raise your inner state of abundance. It becomes easier to believe you can create greater abundance in your life if your senses perceive that the signs of lack and limitation are being reduced. Are you ready to create a positive epidemic of prosperity in your life?

Start by being up front and honest about what you need and expect. The results may surprise you. Whenever you catch yourself saying or thinking "I know I shouldn't, but..." or, "I know I should, but..." stop and reconsider. Then consciously choose to either continue in the direction you were heading with your thoughts, words and actions, or consciously choose to move forward in a new, more positive direction.

Choose to speak right words. *Choose* to think right thoughts. *Choose* to take right action. *Choose* to give thanks with all your words, thoughts and actions. *Choose* to bring your full tithe to your spiritual Source as an offering of your gratitude and thanks.

You cannot truly tithe of your material good while withholding the tithe of your spirit; do not withhold justice, mercy, kindness, love. Turn every thought, word and deed into a selfless tithe. You are the only one who can control your thoughts, words and deeds. You are the only one who has the power to choose something different.

Giving Thanks

Chapter Six: Setting Your Intentions

How do you spend most of your time: worrying or trusting?
Trust *is expecting the best to happen.*
Worry *is expecting the worst to happen.*
What did you really expect *would happen?*

Every August, just before my birthday, I set my intentions for what I want to receive in the coming year. So often, we set our intention about what we want, and then we focus our energy on the fact that we haven't yet received what we want. In August of 2001, I set my intention and expressed my desire to receive $4,000 in cash, gifts or ideas, every day. I determined that I would consciously focus my attention on *where* I was receiving this $4,000 rather than on how much actual money I was receiving.

I allowed myself to be "worth" $4,000 a day, and I chose to receive the $4,000 and let go of any expectation of how those results would be achieved, living each day with a sense of eager anticipation. Like an expectant mother I did not wonder *if* I would give birth; I merely wondered *how and in what form* the new blessing would appear.

When people donated their time to watch my dog, gave me a massage, took me out to dinner, gave me books, spent time sharing ideas with me, etc., I valued those things. Not only did I value them, I placed a value upon them and I recorded that value.

I did the same for ideas that were sparked by circumstances. Something I read, something I

111

heard, something that was divinely passed along to me in meditation. Everything received a value: What could this idea be worth to me? I placed the value on the idea and then immediately took action to follow up (thus putting into motion the energy needed to make that value manifest). When I had an idea for a workshop somewhere for a particular audience, I wrote to the person in charge. When I had a theological idea, I asked questions to guide me in my search and followed where the answers led me. And so on.

I actively saw cash manifesting as well. I did not see $4,000 a day in cash, but the actual income for my company exceeded the amount budgeted that month and my personal income rose as well.

Your desires manifest when you change your attitude—your expectations—to reflect your true self-worth. Your desires manifest when you look for, see and acknowledge the many different forms abundance takes in your life. Let go of your expectations and replace them with a new-found expectancy. Replace your expectations with anticipations. Expectancy is about anticipation. Expectancy transports you from a mindset that wonders "Will I get what I want?" to a mindset that wonders "How will what I want come into my life?" Expectancy incorporates a knowingness. Know that what you desire is coming, and anticipate its arrival with great joy. For 30 days, replace your expectations with anticipations and you will immediately begin to see results in your life.

A woman tithed at my prosperity seminar, and set her intention to have the right and perfect job that would feed her soul and provide her with the income she desired. Within thirty days she had manifested not one but *two* job offers that were exactly what she'd asked for.

A woman manifested an unexpected $9,000 24 hours after realigning her attitude with one of thanksgiving.

A woman tithed $41 at my prosperity workshop and two days later she received a bonus from her job in the amount of $3,900. She had never received a bonus this large in the past and she attributes it to her tithe, since the amount was nearly 100 times what she'd tithed—which is what she set her intentions to receive!

Aligning Your Actions With Your Intentions

Many people use their money with right intention, giving to support causes they care about, even though they do not tithe. Remember: You have no obligation to tithe. You have an opportunity to tithe. You may be perfectly satisfied with all areas of your life and you may see no need to tithe. Spending your money with right intention may be enough for you.

For example, you may buy organic food to support your commitment to environmental values and local producers. You may buy items that are fairly traded in order to support developing countries or you may buy secondhand in order to support recycling. You may also make donations to organizations you support.

Supporting your commitment to your values is a very sound approach to giving and this strategy will draw to you the same energy you are putting out. You will draw to you likeminded people, and you will strengthen your values in these areas. Would you like to provide even greater support to these worthy causes? If so, tithing is the best way I know to increase your abundance so that you have more to share with these worthy causes.

Remember: Tithing is a form of intentional giving. By tithing, you give back to the Universe a portion of what the Universe has given you as a way of saying "Thank you for supporting me in my ventures here on this planet."

Helping support the planet through your purchases is noble and worthy, and it is important to offer the same support to your spiritual Source—in whatever form Spirit moves you—so the planet continues to thrive. For instance, you support a particular artist when you buy their CD or a ticket to their concert. This is not a tithe. This is a gift. However, if you send additional money to that artist, because one of their songs really touched your spirit and fed your soul, that amount would be a tithe. A tithe is a gift of thanksgiving, with no expectation of anything in return. Allow your conscience to be your guide. When you tithe, you're giving to express your thanks for something that fed your spirit with no expectation of anything in return.

Your spiritual Source will appear through many, many channels in your life, just as your good, your abundance, will appear through many channels. Your tithing consciousness will evolve over time, so be patient with the process.

When I first started tithing, I sent money to causes I believed in that helped children, particularly abused children and children who were

114

runaways or throwaways. Even as I gave, I could sense something was missing. So I started tithing to spiritual organizations that I knew were open and receptive to universal approaches to Spirit (such as the local Unitarian-Universalist and Unity churches), even though I had never attended them or been spiritually fed by them.

Once I started really "getting" the premise of tithing—giving back a portion of my good to the spiritual Source from which it came—I started giving to various channels that fed my spirit each week. I would actively watch for places where my soul leaped up and sang for joy because of an encounter with someone, something I read, something I heard, something I saw, and I would tithe to those people immediately. These were people who helped me learn more about myself and my spirituality.

In addition to other places I've already mentioned, I've tithed to churches where I've spoken; I've tithed to waiters whose incredible service late at night nearly brought me to tears; and I've tithed to hotel housekeeping staff for joyously giving me room to work. I've tithed directly to ministers, friends, homeless people, children and so on. I've tithed to organizations that help impoverished children and support global peace efforts.

When you step out in faith and begin tithing a full 10% of your income with gratitude and thanksgiving incredible things begin taking place. Abundance in all areas of your life will appear, and you will be able to give even more to the charitable organizations you cherish. I now give much more to charities from my increased income, above and beyond the 10% that I give as a "thank you" to spiritual channels that feed my soul every day.

As I said before, your tithing consciousness will evolve over time. Only you can determine where you're comfortable tithing. If you're concerned or worried or uncomfortable with where you're tithing, then I recommend engaging in my **Conscious Tithing** exercise for 90 days, so you can learn how to tap into the true power of tithing.

Here's how **Conscious Tithing** works. Mark off 90 days on the calendar. During the next 90 days, practice the art of tithing by giving away 10% of whatever income you receive each day, with immense gratitude, to someone who feeds your spirit. It could be a homeless man on the corner who suddenly lifts you out of a blue mood, because you realize how insignificant your problems are compared to his today. It could be a child whose innocence brings a smile to your face. It could be a writer who brings you an "Aha!" moment with his writing. It could be a musician whose song helps you heal. It could be a waitress whose kind demeanor brightens your day. It could be an organization whose commitment to their cause makes you feel hopeful about the future of the human race. It could be a minister or a church whose spiritual message gives you the strength you needed to do what you thought you couldn't do.

Do not prejudge who you're tithing to or where you're tithing. Do not use your tithe to "feed need." Wherever your spirit is fed, whomever feeds your soul, tithe to them. Take the income you receive that day (or the day before, which is easier to do since you already know how much that was!) and give away 10% of it, on the spot. Tithe the 10% and give thanks for the blessings in your life. The day you start your 90-day period, write down your current income and your current financial situation. Each day, record the gifts and blessings you receive, the things you're grateful for and the income and unexpected gifts (tangible and intangible) that come to you. In addition, during those 90 days, write down any thoughts and feelings that come up for you about the act of tithing.

At the end of the 90 days, check to see what has changed in your finances, in the other areas of your life, and in the way you think and feel about tithing. I know you'll be pleasantly surprised.

> A woman was worried about being able to sell her home quickly. She tithed and set her intention to sell her home, at the right and perfect price to the right and perfect people, within 30 days. She then began taking action as she was guided to do. She started by cleaning out the house, then determined what she wanted to do to get the house ready for sale. Everything she asked for came to her effortlessly, even things that had proved difficult in the past. She had determined the house would find its new owners, who would be the right and perfect people. Her Realtor said the strangest thing happened when the new owners first saw the house: The wife felt she just had to have that very house. None other would do.

What major goal have you been trying to accomplish? Set your intention today and start tithing to give thanks for the good that already exists in your life, then take the steps to bring you toward your goal. I guarantee you'll accomplish your goal before you know it.

A man knew that tithing worked, but for several months he resisted giving thanks and had become downright lazy in sending his tithes to his spiritual organization. He eventually sent a check and a month later received a pay raise. He then began to tithe 10% of whatever cash he had at the end of the day, depositing it in the ATM of the local bank, so he could write out a tithe check to his spiritual organization each month. The very next day, he received another check from his employer giving him another substantial monthly raise.

His part-time Reiki practice also began taking off. Substantial amounts of money were manifested in his bank accounts, and he was able to pay important bills and honor checks he had written.

Setting your intention to tithe is a powerful step, which can begin to manifest greater good in your life even before you begin to send out the tithe. Be very cautious, however, if you decide to save up your tithes in order to give monthly. It's very easy for our egos to get in the way and look at the money we've set aside and decide, "Oh, it's not quite enough yet to tithe" or "This is far too much to tithe!" or "I'll tithe part of it now but save part of it in case something comes up I need it for."

A first time tither's faith was immediately rewarded. He had the best sales week he'd ever had, even though sales were down for everyone else in the company. His commission check was over $4,000, and his boss told him he wanted to talk with him about a promotion. Everything he touched seemed to turn to gold.

When he sat down to tithe, he realized his tithe check would be over $400 and he began to wonder what else he could be doing with that $400. He decided to use that money to pay bills instead of paying his tithe.

Suddenly, his income stream dried up, clients were hesitant to buy, and his boss kept delaying their scheduled meeting regarding his promotion.

When he realized he had stopped up the flow by withholding his tithe, he panicked, because he no longer had $400 to tithe. He did, however, have an abundance of self-help books. I recommended that he go through his bookshelves and tithe $400 worth of books to a men's shelter or other organization to help other people get back on their feet. Once he did, the abundance in his own life began to effortlessly flow again.

It's also equally important to tithe of your thoughts, as well as to tithe of your time, talents and treasures. Be on guard against the subconscious roadblocks you may set up on your own road to abundance. If you find yourself rationalizing why it's not necessary to give your tithe, immediately ask yourself what is scaring you.

When you are hesitant to tithe of your thoughts, words or actions, you may find that old relationship issues are coming up for you. You may be fearful that someone will take advantage of you, or you may not trust someone to support you and not hurt you.

When you're hesitant to tithe of your treasures, you may find that old money issues are coming up for you. Our relationships with money are very complicated and are based on what we learned about money—consciously or

119

subconsciously—when we were children. If you are looking to explore your own money issues, I recommend reading my **Seven Commitments to Healing Your Relationship With Money**. One of the biggest issues that surfaces for most people around money is control.

We are uncomfortable not "knowing" that the tithe we give is creating greater abundance in our lives. Unlike the money we send to a creditor, which immediately reduces or pays off a bill, a tithe generally has no direct, tangible result we can immediately point to as evidence of our prosperity.

We may tithe our words out of kindness to someone and receive a short-tempered reply in return. It is tempting to throw in the towel when this occurs, but I encourage you to let go of the immediate appearances and continue to tithe of your thoughts, words and actions.

Releasing Control

To have and not to give is often worse than to steal.
— Marie von Ebner-Eschenbach

We all like to feel we individually control our destiny. Because of this, when things start going well, we tell God, "Okay, thanks for the directions. I'll take over from here." Then, as conductors of our own life's train, we stop listening as God tries to tell us, "Hey, you, wake up! The bridge up ahead is out." We're so busy explaining to God how we've got everything under control that we overlook the warning signs and signals the Universe sends our way, including the helping hands that try to point us in the right direction.

When things are going well, we feel in control. Then, as things start to get out of control and fall apart, our thoughts, words and actions suddenly shift. We begin to get frustrated. We begin focusing our attention on the problem instead of on what we desire. We start blaming others, trying to fix the problem by ourselves and forgetting we had help in "pulling it all together."

To keep from getting off track, or to get back on track if your attitude of thanksgiving becomes derailed, mentally go through your day and count your blessings, even in your head as you're going off to sleep. "Count your many blessings, name them one by one" as the children's song says. At the end of every day, let the last thoughts you have be about all the ways you are thankful for how Spirit has moved in your life that day, so your first thoughts in the morning will be thankful thoughts on how Spirit will move in your life during the day that has just dawned.

> A woman practiced the art of tithing faith-
> fully for quite some time and saw it working in
> her life. Then she started calling it success and
> thought she was responsible for what she had and
> for creating more. The further she strayed from
> abundant thinking and gratitude for her bounty,
> the more complicated her life became, even
> though she continued to tithe. She eventually
> forgot how to be abundant, until one day she
> realized what she was doing to herself and her
> family. She looked around at the gifts in her life
> and took time to appreciate and enjoy them. She

saw with wonderment and surprise that she had a beautiful life and a beautiful family. She had forgotten how truly blessed she was.

Since moving back to actively practicing gratitude and abundance, she has experienced immediate changes in her life. She considers it a gift from the Universe that, once she recognized her role in keeping abundance and gratitude out of her life, reminders and quiet lessons have dropped into her lap from everywhere, gently guiding her back on the path.

A spiritual leader related a story of two people who wanted the last space at a seminar. One person had financial means and was trying to bargain, wanting to pay $500, a sizeable discount on the seminar cost. The second person only had $20. When asked who he chose, he replied, "The one who was willing to give everything he had." Where are your thoughts focused? Are your thoughts focused on *getting* as much as you can, or on *giving* as much as you can?

You will always get whatever you are willing to give. You cannot expect to get more unless you're first willing to give more. For example, you cannot expect to get better service from someone unless you are willing to give better service as a customer. Remember: tithing involves our thoughts, words and actions. We cannot expect to have greater joy in our lives if we aren't first willing to tithe with our thoughts and words as willingly and cheerfully as we tithe with our actions.

One day, I stopped to pump gas while on a long trip home. The machine wouldn't respond properly to my request to pay inside, so I pressed the button for assistance. I could see the two employees inside, chatting and laughing, but the machine continued to say "please wait" and no assistance came. I could feel myself getting frustrated. I was tired and still had hours to drive.

Finally, a clerk stuck her head out the door and asked if I wanted to pay with cash. I stopped myself from being surly and simply said "Yes, but the machine isn't responding." She walked over, mashed two buttons and then turned to me and smiled. She apologized for the problem, and told me to have a great day. My ego instantly deflated. I was grateful I hadn't snapped at her for my assumption that she didn't care about me, her customer.

I wanted to be recognized as a valued customer. When I made the assumption that I wasn't being valued, I withheld the tithe of my spirit, the tithe of my thoughts and had rude thoughts instead. I recognized the thoughts and chose to make my actions kinder and more compassionate. Because I valued the clerk with my actions, she in turn valued me with her words and actions.

Too often our egos get tied up in our giving, and our giving becomes a source of personal recognition instead of pure giving for the sake of giving thanks. If you notice that the flow of your prosperity becomes blocked, begin practicing the **Conscious Tithing** exercise in every way you tithe, to check if your ego is getting involved in your tithing efforts. If so, take steps to release the money or the resentment or the need for recognition as soon as possible.

A woman in real estate practiced affirmations regularly and had seen them work countless times in the past, yet the flow of prosperity in her life had become stagnant. So she began being more conscious with her tithes. She released unwanted treasures and forgave a $4,000 debt to her brother, but she was unable to move forward financially.

She took the matter into reflection and realized that when she met her husband, her business took off like crazy, and she was surrounded with positive energy. This all changed after she moved into his home; her business went downhill. During her reflection, her stepdaughter, with whom she had an antagonistic relationship, instantly came to mind.

The woman began saying affirmations that would free her from her stepdaughter's presence. The affirmations, though filled with words of release, were also filled with resentment. Every time she practiced her affirmations, her stepdaughter would stop coming to her home and the woman's business picked up. Eventually, her stepdaughter stopped coming over permanently. When this happened, the woman's business dried up completely.

She continued saying business-building affirmations. Each affirmation was said with feeling and ended with the woman claiming her good and thanking the Universe, yet she still felt stuck. She hadn't released the resentment and therefore never truly gave her tithe with thanksgiving.

Disharmony in your home can cause the flow of good in your life to dwindle. If you find yourself in a situation where there is any disharmony in your home, you'll need to open up the channels of communication in the situation if you want greater abundance to come to you. You must discover what energy is still swirling around you in regard to the issue that is causing disharmony. You may find a deep-seated but unspoken anger, fear, resentment or sadness exists where love should exist instead.

While you can never change someone else's behavior, you can change your own behavior and you can send out energy of forgiveness. Claim responsibility for and acknowledge your role in the disharmony and then release the situation to its highest good for all concerned. An excellent forgiveness affirmation is: *"I forgive and am forgiven for all past thoughts, words and deeds in this situation and I bless and support everyone involved in all their power and magnificence. Thank you, God!"*

Finding the Freedom in Forgiveness

Human freedom involves our capacity to pause,
to choose the one response toward which we wish to throw our weight.

— Marie von Ebner-Eschenbach

A woman once contacted me because she kept receiving tithes of $77. She wondered if there was some significance to the figure. I explained to her to that, metaphysically, the number seven represents fullness and perfection. We have the seven wonders of the world, the seven chakras, the seven senses (sight, sound, taste, smell, touch, intuition and telepathy). Seventy times seven carries even more power. This is the number that implies unlimited forgiveness, about which Jesus spoke. A vital step toward creating a life of abundance is mastering the art of forgiveness.

True forgiveness is offered up with gratitude and thankfulness for the role the events have played in helping you express your highest good in your life. Good will flow to you like never before when you open up the door to forgiveness. Wherever you are feeling stuck, look for the bottleneck of what has yet to be forgiven. You may find what has not been forgiven lurking in the corner, with a cover draped over it, because you thought keeping it out of sight would keep it out of mind. You may find that the disharmony has been hidden away behind a big red brick wall you've built to protect yourself from the pain of dealing with the issue. You cannot push away disharmony, or put it out of sight. It takes more energy to keep disharmony covered up than it does to heal it.

> A woman who had a lifelong dream was frustrated. She felt like a decade of attempts to fulfill her dream had been stymied by people who were jealous of her talents and by events that she took as personal rejection. I had her make a list of everyone she felt had ever held her back professionally. She meticulously listed everyone, and then made a list of why she was thankful for that person or situation—what she had learned, what gifts she had gained from that experience or encounter. One by one, she released her resentments by thanking them all for their contributions, which had brought her to where she was right now, professionally. Six months after forgiving them and releasing her resentments, she was well on her way to fulfilling her lifelong dream!

How many times shall you forgive someone? According to the biblical story (Matthew 18:22), true forgiveness comes when you forgive someone seventy times seven times, meaning: when you forgive someone abundantly. Forgiveness is simpler than we often make it out to be. Forgiving someone means making a conscious choice to let go of the pain, to let go of the need to be right, and to allow yourself to heal and to be happy instead. Forgiveness is an act of consciously seeing everyone blessed for their highest good in the situation that is grieving you. Embrace the number seven and the principle of forgiveness, giving forth your good toward others. The powerful impact on your life cannot be underestimated.

To restore the flow of harmony and abundance in any area of your life, you must claim responsibility for your role and give and seek forgiveness (in that order) from all concerned. Do you ever wait for someone else to apologize first, even though you have the desire to apologize? When you do this, you're withholding the tithe of your words. Somehow you fear that you will lose respect, or lose face, or lose power in the situation that occurred. Remember: nothing can ever be lost; it can only be converted.

A man was attending church one Sunday when a modern-day prophet stood up to deliver a message, saying God told him to tell whomever was in turmoil about a $20,000 debt that the debt had been forgiven. The man who had carried the indebtedness stood up, crying. The $20,000 was the amount of his unpaid tithes.

Anytime you feel anxious about the flow of abundance in your life, check in with yourself. Ask yourself: "Do I have enough for today?" Not for what you need tomorrow, or the next day, or for what is due next week or next month. Do you have enough for *today*?

You may wish to use a reminder affirmation to keep your thoughts focused on the truth about the abundance in your life. One helpful affirmation I highly recommend is: *I now have enough time, energy, wisdom, love and money to accomplish all that I need to accomplish today, Thank You, God!* The best affirmations always begin or end with the words *Thank you, God.*

When you find yourself speaking words of limitation, convincing yourself you live paycheck to paycheck, or your relationship can't be salvaged, or the energy you have right now is going to run out, use an affirmation to stop your thoughts from drifting away from your connection to abundance.

You can use an affirmation as simple as *What God has given, cannot be diminished.* Another excellent affirmation is simply: *This is all for my highest good. Everything is unfolding in Divine Order, in Divine Timing. All is well.*

> A woman was in line to receive an inheritance of $40,000 a year, which would come from a trust fund administered by her and two other trustees. Because she did not have complete control over how the funds would be dispersed to her, she became afraid that she wouldn't have what she needed when she needed it. Because she did not have complete control over how the inheritance would be paid out to her, she did something amazing.
>
> She turned down the inheritance.

Imagine yourself in that situation. Would you turn down your inheritance? If not, then why do you turn down your Divine Inheritance? Become open and receptive to receiving unlimited abundance in your life today. Start by establishing a firm practice of tithing so that you are already giving thanks for the manifestation of your divine inheritance. Then release your expectations of how that inheritance will appear in your life.

Remember: You set your intentions with your thoughts and words, as well as with your deeds. Set your intention to embrace your Divine Inheritance right here, right now.

Giving Thanks

Chapter Seven: The Etiquette of Tithing

There is no such thing as charity as popularly understood.
Everything belongs to God
and all His children are equally entitled to it.
— Charles Fillmore

Tithing raises many questions and pushes many buttons for people. An on-going debate rages over whether tithing is necessary or whether giving to the needy is a more appropriate way to give in today's times. This creates the illusion that giving or receiving a tithe is an act of charity. So many people have a visceral negative reaction to being "a charity case." In fact, the thought of being a charity case keeps many of us from openly receiving our good. Just as there is an art to tithing, there is also an etiquette to tithing that will provide you with some guidelines to help you work past these obstacles to giving and receiving. Once you work past these obstacles, you can fully embrace your good.

For starters, some people believe that the New Testament of the Bible does away with tithing or that the tithe has been replaced by "a glad offering" or by free will offerings. It is not my intent to dissuade them, or you, from your beliefs. I merely wish to point out that the difference may merely be one of semantics. If you find you have a visceral reaction to the word "tithe," stop and examine where this reaction is coming from. You may discover you carry around outdated beliefs about tithing, beliefs that are tied to control issues, which I addressed in the previous chapter.

If you have manifested everything you desire in all areas of your life, and you have great joy in all areas of your life, by giving in a way that resonates strongly with you, then keep doing what you're doing. Whatever name you call the gifts you give freely, cheerfully, joyfully and willingly, keep giving them with grateful thanksgiving and you will find yourself firmly in the flow of your abundance.

As you begin practicing the art of tithing—no matter what name you call it—you'll soon discover that what goes around comes around. As you give, so shall you receive. Which is why learning to be a better receiver is such an important part of tithing. Every time you receive, you make it possible for ten times that amount to come back to both you and the giver. You bless the giver's tithe when you receive with gratitude and thanksgiving by acknowledging the gift. When people give to you, it is because they place great value on you!

Learning to be a better receiver is as important as learning how to be a better giver. Become open and receptive to receiving the good that comes to you, by making a mental shift in how you view tithes. Many people (and I admit to being one of them when I first began tithing!) view tithes as charity or some sort of handout, which we view negatively.

The meaning of words and phrases evolve over time. The quote at the beginning of this chapter will hopefully help you reframe the popular meaning of charity. *"There is no such thing as charity, as popularly understood. Everything belongs to God and all His children are equally entitled to it."* No one is asking for a handout, and you're not giving a handout when you give a tithe. Likewise, you're not receiving a handout, if you're the recipient of a tithe.

132

You are simply receiving part of the good that God has prepared for you.

Charity, being benevolent, means doing good or causing good to be done. Our history is filled with "benefactors" who created trust funds or otherwise supported artists, musicians, composers, writers, teachers, ministers, rabbis, so that they might be free to minister to the masses, according to their talents and missions. These acts of charity brought attention to and provided support for the creative and spiritual work these individuals were doing. Today, much of this benevolent work is done through tax-deductible charities, but much is also still done through individuals with no thought to the tax benefit or any other benefit.

> An old Buddhist story tells about a merchant who gave a monk a bag of gold for the improvement of the local monastery. The monk acknowledged the gift, and nothing more. The merchant, expecting gratitude, was consternated that none was forthcoming. After hinting to the unresponsive monk for a short while, he finally burst out and said, "I just gave you an entire bag of gold! I would think someone who just received such a gift would be thankful!" To which the monk replied with a big grin, "I just accepted a bag of gold. The giver should be thankful."

It's easy to find ourselves expecting an outpouring of verbal gratitude and thanksgiving from those who receive our gifts and tithes. Be on guard when these expectations arise. Remember that tithing is about giving thanks for what we have already been given. It's not about giving in order to get, whether what we're expecting to get is someone's favor, preferential treatment, or merely a "thank you."

Practice tithing with everything you give. I've talked to many people who have stopped giving gifts to different relatives, simply because they never received a thank you note from the recipient. Proper etiquette indicates that a thank you note or call regarding a gift is appropriate, but not receiving a thank you is not a reason to withhold your gifts and tithes. When you do that, you're withholding your gift because you didn't receive: you're giving in order to get a thank you note, not as a way of giving thanks. This simple act takes you out of the flow of your good.

Stay in the Constant Flow

Just as you should be careful not to block your prosperity by withholding your tithes and gifts, don't let others take your prosperity away by allowing them to refuse your tithe.

> I'm often moved by incredible music. The first time I tithed directly to the soloist and the pianist at my home church, they both attempted to turn down the tithe. I simply said, "Please don't stand in the way of my prosperity. You fed my soul and I feel compelled to give you this gift. Please accept it graciously in the spirit in which it is being given." These simple words of thanks carried a profound message.

People often turn down tithes because they are afraid of appearing needy and because we've had it drummed into our heads that we don't accept charity, or money, for doing good deeds. Doing the good deed is supposed to be reward enough. And it is. Accepting a tithe is another good deed.

Accepting a gift is as much a blessing to the giver as the gift is to the receiver. Giving a tithe or receiving a tithe isn't about balancing the books; it's about maintaining the flow of abundance in your life through a conscious act of giving thanks.

Tap into the circular flow of tithing energy. Energy must flow in, around and through you or it becomes stagnant. This goes for money energy as well as any other kind of energy. You must give freely and receive freely or you will put a bottleneck in the universal flow of energy. You stop up your own abundance and that of those around you when you react to a tithe from a place of fear or shame, whether you're giving or receiving.

When you give, it's equally important to stay open and receptive to the gifts of time, talent and treasures that are offered to you. Tithes, donations, gifts, kind words—whatever you call the blessings shared by others from their income, their time or their unique abilities—are acts of good.

I recommend a simple exercise if you are uncomfortable receiving a tithe. If someone is tithing to you and you're worried they are giving too large an amount, or too expensive an item, or too much of their time, or you're afraid there's a string attached to the gift simply ask: "Are you sure?" If they say "Yes" then say "Thank You" and graciously accept their tithe so that all may prosper. I was once part of an unusual tithing situation that illustrates this concept.

> I spent some time with my wonderful
> spiritual mentor, Nellie Lauth, and tithed to her.
> Later that evening, I received a tithe from Nellie. I
> was so grateful for the unexpected tithe, and for
> how deeply I was moved during that evening's
> meditation which Nellie led, that I immediately
> tithed back to Nellie 10% of what I had just
> received.

Sometimes, you will find that you spiritually feed each other. Honor that with your tithes. Don't withhold your tithes because you think it's "weird" to tithe back to someone who just tithed to you. At the same time, do not feel obligated to give back to someone who has given to you, unless they have fed your spirit, and you wish to thank them in kind.

It's time to begin to acknowledge that you are always tithing, all day, whether you know it or not. You tithe of your talents, even in your everyday work world. You tithe of your thoughts, every time you rejoice in someone else's good. You tithe of your words, every time you offer someone encouragement. You tithe of your treasure, every time you joyfully spend money on something.

Give your tithes freely, with gratitude and thanksgiving, and stay open and receptive to the good that will be coming to you. This good may come in the form of a steady paycheck, a desired weight loss, a new client, an unexpected opportunity, wonderful gifts or a joyous relationship. Be open and receptive to letting Spirit decide how your good will come to you. Release the fear and open your heart to give and receive your tithes.

As you become more in tune with the flow of Universal Abundance, your good will begin to appear in your life in a multitude of ways. Don't turn down the good that appears in your life as charity. People will begin to do things for you, or give you things, and you need to learn how to graciously receive them.

> A middle-aged couple had been tithing for months and they called to say that their finances were in worse shape than they were before they started tithing. I asked them to walk me through what had been happening in their lives over the past few months. The husband told of how his sister had taken their children out to lunch and had later wanted to take the entire family out to dinner, but he said she couldn't because she had already bought lunch. Then the wife told of how her in-laws had offered to sit down with them to go over their finances and give them some money to help them through their dry spell, but they hadn't taken the in-laws up on the offer, because they assumed the in-laws couldn't really afford to give them money.
> All sorts of incredible prosperity opportunities and gifts had been unfolding in their lives, and they had refused to recognize and accept them. When they mentioned their realization to their helpful relatives, the relatives were quick to point out many other ways the couple had been turning down their good!

Above all else, have faith. Have faith in the goodness of the work you are doing, in the goodness of the community around you that will support you and your work, and in your own innate goodness. Give back to God a portion of your good and God will see you are committed to bringing forth more good. Then, make known what you desire in your life. Set your intentions and ask God for exactly what you need.

What kind of lifestyle do you desire to support you and your family in comfort, doing work that you love? Make your request, and give thanks in advance that what you desire is yours.

The Art of Receiving

Argue for your limitations and, sure enough, they're yours.
— Richard Bach

Are you ready to begin asking the Universe for what you want and trusting that you will receive it or do you want to continue to believe that you shouldn't expect more, that it's not right to expect more than what you have?

A woman had no money in the bank, no cash on hand and no food for lunch one day. She had credit cards, but didn't want to rely on them. Instead, she decided to trust God for her lunch. At lunchtime, she was still waiting expectantly wondering how her lunch would manifest. She did not wonder *if* it would manifest. She simply wondered *how*. Would someone offer to take her to lunch or give her their leftovers or what? A half hour into her lunch break she decided, for fun, to go through her wallet just to see what was there. No money, as she thought, just credit cards. But then, she found a gift certificate for a FREE meal at a local chicken place. She was so delighted with her little miracle she laughed out loud.

138

An abundance of "coincidences" surrounded a workshop tour of mine. Any time we needed, wanted or desired anything, we asked out loud for it, and it manifested. We received hotel rooms at specific prices, a glass of Merlot and live music after a long day (which manifested at a *diner* of all places), incredible food, an abundance of cash instead of checks (so we wouldn't have to find a bank to cash a check), and the right and perfect people attending our seminars.

We became so used to getting everything we asked for that we would just ask out loud and then give it no more thought for the rest of the day—knowing positively that we were going to get what we asked for. We had no fear of not having enough. There was only a complete knowing that the Universe would provide.

Ask and expect to receive. What are you going to ask for? What do you truly desire in your life? And how can you build enough trust to know that you'll receive it in divine timing?

Don't limit yourself. A woman once gifted me with an all-expense-paid two-week trip to Hawaii as a tithe for my services. Before we got off the phone, she asked, "Is there anything else you need today?" Without thinking, I immediately reverted to limited thinking and said "Oh, no, you've done quite enough already."

Here someone was willingly, cheerfully and joyfully extending a tithe and I batted it down without a moment's thought, because I assumed they were asking out of politeness and not because they were offering me a part of my limitless abundance. I learned never to make assumptions, and to always receive tithes cheerfully.

A regular tither demonstrated the prospering power of affirmative prayers when she sat down and began writing out the affirmation *"Everything and everybody prospers me now."* She had written it four times when a co-worker came by and handed her a $25 Petsmart gift card which she used to get her dog's nails clipped and buy him some toys and treats.

Receiving through giving is a paradox of tithing. When you give, you naturally open yourself up to receive.

The minister of a severely indebted church suggested that his church members tithe. His suggestion was soundly voted down. He then asked that they try tithing for one month. At month's end, those who heartily entered into the agreement and were giving thanks with their tithes were prospering abundantly. Those who grudgingly tithed admitted they had held their own. The members agreed to tithe another six months, at which point the church was debt-free and had begun saving money.

A single mother with four children tithed from her first minimum wage paycheck. As she continued tithing, her salary increased. One year later, her monthly salary had increased to nearly eight times her original salary.

A contractor tithed faithfully and his business was always booming. Another contractor on his block did equally good work but didn't believe in tithing. He rarely had enough work to stay busy and often hired himself out to his neighbor. The only apparent difference between the two men was that one gave thanks with his tithe and one did not.

One man began tithing ten dollars a month and continued tithing as his income grew. When his tithe grew to one hundred dollars a month, this seemed too much to tithe and he stopped tithing altogether. Disaster followed in all areas of his life until he again began to tithe.

Setting Your Intentions

Don't pray for more—
pray for a greater awareness of how the omnipresent abundance of the Universe is manifest in your life, here and now.
— Paula Langguth Ryan (oh, wait, that's me!)

Getting into the flow of things and realizing that everything is working out perfectly (even when it doesn't match *our* idea of what *perfect* is supposed to be) is one of the highest changes in consciousness any of us can reach. As you give, so shall you receive. Give not out of guilt or fear, but give in whatever way you're spiritually led to give. When you receive, focus on receiving out of love, gratitude and thankfulness and not out of guilt or fear. When you do, you will discover that the bounty of gifts available from the Universe is limitless. Large and small demonstrations will abound as you give thanks with your tithes and take your place in the never-ending flow of abundance by gratefully receiving all the abundance that is offered to you.

141

Here's a sampling of the abundance that was offered to people who contacted me during just one two-week period:

- free tickets to "The Big E," New England's fair
- a large bagful of thermal underwear
- free raspberries, potatoes, beets, tomatoes, squash and pickles
- free auto parts (this particularly excited me because it was the first time this new tither recognized the results of her tithing!)
- a free salad
- free dresses
- a $417 discount on new brakes
- free massages
- potted plants
- hot apple cider
- thousands of dollars of technical computer support
- free honey
- free ironing
- a free modem card
- free books
- free music
- spiritual breakthroughs
- an outpouring of creative ideas
- free dog food, dog care and boarding
- healing relationships with loved ones
- discounts on rental equipment
- new clients
- effortless interactions with people who seemed to go out of their way to prosper them

- unexpected income
- free Mets tickets (a gift everyone but Yankee fans would appreciate!)
- the resolution of an ongoing financial challenge
- peace of mind about current stock market investments
 the perfect dinner companion and so much more!

By giving, you open yourself up to receive. And by being willing to receive you create an incredible circulation of good in all areas of your life.

Once you're ready and willing to receive greater good in your life, write down what you desire in the form of an intention. See yourself having what you desire, and know that how your desire manifests in your life is always for your highest good. I recommend ending your intention with the phrase *"This or something better, and so it is, for the highest good of all. Thank you, God!"*

Below, I've listed some sample intentions for different areas of your life, which will help you set your intentions. Many of these are actual intentions that my students have held in prayer, to manifest what they desired in their lives.

Following Your Life Purpose/Releasing Fear

I see myself open and receptive to the knowledge that God, and only God, is the source of my good!

I see my highest good revealed to me!

143

I see myself joyfully sharing my blessings with all I encounter!

I see everyone effortlessly supporting me!

I see myself stepping out in faith, releasing all fear and doubt, and embracing the love that I deserve and desire, from myself and from others!

I see myself on track in every area of my life, as I become open and receptive to the knowledge that i deserve all the abundance that flows to me!

I see myself at peace with the unfolding of events!

All that I desire now comes to me, in divine order, as I make myself open and receptive, giving and receiving love in all areas of my life!

I see myself examining, understanding, embracing and effortlessly living my truth!

I see myself secure and at peace!

144

I see myself blessed with the knowledge needed to manifest my heart's desires!

I see myself open and receptive to my heart's desires!

I see myself fully embracing my divine knowledge, secure in the knowledge that all my desires are mine already— waiting for me to claim my good now!

I see myself in the right and perfect place in my life!

I see myself open and receptive to embracing myself and my life fully, in divine timing!

I see everything in my life unfolding in divine timing!

I see myself released from my fears and doubts!

Relationships of All Types

I see myself ever blessed, loved and loving in all my interactions with others!

I see the right and perfect romantic relationship manifesting in my life now as I make myself open and receptive to giving and receiving love in all areas of my life!

I see myself having the wedding of my dreams at the right and perfect price!

I see myself open and receptive to healing my relationship now!

I see myself released from all fears, able and willing to communicate lovingly and openly to resolve existing relationship issues and create a lasting, loving partnership now!

I see myself open and receptive to being of right service to all those whose lives cross my path!

I see myself releasing and blessing all those who I misperceive to have caused me harm. As I forgive, I give, and as I give, I receive a multitude of blessings!

I see myself inspired and creative, and able to put my ideas into form as I interact with others!

I see the right and perfect relationship manifesting in my life now as I step out in faith and become the perfect partner I wish to have in my life!

I freely and fully forgive everyone in all past relationships, including myself. I am open and receptive to receiving the right and perfect relationship now!

Debt Free and Prosperous Living

I see myself freely giving and receiving from the bounty that the Universe is providing me with now!

I see myself incurring no debt for what I desire, with everything falling into place effortlessly, in divine timing, in divine order!

I see myself open and receptive to receiving $10,000 worth of abundance or more, now, as I become open and receptive to the knowledge that I deserve all the abundance that flows to me!

I see my savings and investments growing effortlessly, every day, building the right and perfect nest egg for me!

I see myself firmly planted in the flow of peace and prosperity!

I see all my finances in perfect order now!

I see my financial situation improving easiky and effortlessly, every day!

I see myself ever prospered in all I do!

I see myself released from my fears and my debts!

I see myself current with all my bills and rapidly paying off all my debts!

I see myself owing no one anything but love!

I see myself completely free from all my debts!

I see myself released from all obligations to others as I release all others from their obligations to me, seeing them ever prospered by God!

Transitions

I see my move as a prosperous and abundant move, in all ways!

I see myself in the right and perfect new home!

I see myself embracing the good that is in my life today, making room for the greater good that is to come!

I see myself as a free spirit, welcoming change!

I see myself living peacefuly with the chaos around me, trusting in the process!

I see myself selling my home effortlessly, for the right and perfect price!

I see the right and perfect outcome to this situation unfolding in my life now!

Career/Business

I see the right and perfect opportunity coming to me now, in divine timing!

149

I see myself effortlessly and joyfully receiving my new success and my increased income in a positive way, using my greater good to bless others as I too have been blessed!

I see myself stepping out in faith to do the work I love, secure in the knowledge that all my needs will be met, abundantly!

I see myself in a fulfilling and prosperous job!

I see myself excelling in my new work!

I see my new business growing effortlessly and prosperously!

I see happy customers effortlessly drawn to my positive energy and my attitude of service!

I see an endless stream of referrals coming to me now!

I see my business growing effortlessly every day, in every way, as I open myself up to the divine flow of good that is fully present in my life!

I see myself open receptive and ready to step out in faith, releasing my attachment to my job as the source of my good!

I see people effortlessly drawn to me, valuing me and my work and prospering me now!

Health and Vitality

I see myself whole, healed and healthy, in all areas of my life!

I see every area of my life in complete balance now, with an abundance of time to workout, meditate and relax!

I see myself filled with divine light, energy, peace, love and joy!

I see the right and perfect healing manifesting in my life now!

I see my body as flexible and strong, and I delight in my vibrant health!

I see myself releasing weight rapidly, permanently and in a healthy manner!

This or something better now manifests for the highest good of all. And so it is. Thank you, God!

In my role as a prosperity coach, people often write me with their intentions. I hold their intention in prayer for 30 days, then write to see what has manifested in their lives.

Are you ready to set your intention for what you desire? Write out your intention and send me a copy. I'll gladly hold your intention in prayer for you for 30 days. The power of prayer is always magnified whenever two or more people are gathered in prayer.

Intentions may be sent to:
Paula Langguth Ryan c/o The Art of Abundance
1121 Annapolis Road, Suite 120, Odenton, MD 21113
Or via email at: PaulaRyan@artofabundance.com

Chapter Eight:
Expanding Your View of Prosperity

Everything and everybody prospers me now.
— Catherine Ponder

Practicing the art of tithing in all areas of your life means being prepared for incredible wisdom, success, health, joy, love, financial wealth and an outpouring of abundance in all areas of your life. Are you ready? Can you conceive of *having* more good in your life, or are you trapped in the cycle of *wishing* you had more good in your life?

How would you react if you suddenly found your income doubling this month? What would you do with your newfound income? How would you change? How would you react if you suddenly had everything you ever wanted, right now, and if any need or desire that came up was fulfilled instantly? How strong are your values? Would you continue to hold onto your scarcity models of what your life can look like? Would you always be waiting for the other shoe to drop? Or would you expand your feelings about abundance beyond anything that you could possibly imagine for yourself?

These are very serious questions. I encourage you to stop a moment, grab a pad of paper and write down your answers to the above questions.

Many people have problems being receptive to gifts, no matter how sincere, because they fear there are strings attached.

You may think that such gifts mean you will "owe them one." You may have even grown up in an environment where you believed gifts were given with strings attached. Regardless of the intentions of the giver, you can still receive with a full heart.

> A man who came to this new understanding was able to start unblocking things he didn't even know were blocked. With his newfound understanding of receiving, he accepted an offer from a co-worker who took him out for lunch one day, out of the blue. As a result, he gained a lot of insight about how his co-worker's department worked that he wouldn't have gotten otherwise.

You too can use this information about receiving on your own intellectual and emotional blocks to open up new channels of good. When you do this, you turn those blocks into stepping stones on your new pathway of prosperity. Think about stepping stones a minute.

Each stone, by itself, is fairly useless; ugly, gray—an obstacle. Harness the stones' energy by putting them all together, however, and you can build many things of beauty: a stone fence, bench, pathway, or even the foundation for a waterfall.

The beauty of a stepping stone is in how you perceive it. It's time to start seeing the intellectual and emotional blocks you're dealing with as individual stepping stones on your road to progress instead of as roadblocks. We go through so much of our lives in a state of conscious unconsciousness.

Without these stepping stones—these perceived roadblocks—we would never be jostled into examining our present circumstances and beliefs to see what still holds true for us and what we need to replace in our lives.

A woman who tithes regularly began feeling a prosperity pinch—and it was pinching enough that it hurt a bit. I reminded her of the prosperity basics and reminded her that King Solomon, the richest and wisest man in the Bible, never asked God for money or things, only divine ideas! She then took her challenge into prayer and meditation. That evening she began having very inspired ideas about freeing up the prosperity flow in her life with wonderful tangible results that occurred within a few weeks.

These included:
- a house clearing which dramatically changed the energy in her home
- an unexpected check for $500 from a relative
- the gift of over $100 worth of herbal tinctures for detoxification and draining which she had wanted to purchase but thought she couldn't afford
- the reclaiming of a "junk" room in her house which has become a sanctuary for her
- the most amazing chocolate chip cookies improved communications with almost everyone in her life, and
- a crystal sense of clarity about issues that blocked effective communications in her other relationships.

She also benefited from the movement of hundreds of dollars worth of products she had been "holding onto." She also had a renewed experience of creativity in her life which inspired her to create new classes and co-create teaching opportunities which became opportunities to create new products. Finally, she experienced an incredible sense of limitless love and boundless possibilities in her life.

These all became stepping stones that raised her awareness and caused her to recommit to remembering that we are always in the flow despite what appearances might indicate. Through this experience she came to truly believe that her abundance encompasses so much more than her bank account balance.

Ideas may be the most profitable gift you will ever receive, once you begin giving thanks with your tithes. You will soon discover that, like King Solomon, you need to ask for guidance instead of asking for a specific amount of cash. Instead of giving you fish, God teaches you how to fish. Instead of giving you an immediate cash infusion (although this does happen), you may find that your prosperity comes in the form of new and wonderful ideas that flow to you. Take one step at a time to put those ideas into action.

A woman began tithing again after reading my *Art of Abundance* newsletter and discovered firsthand how tithing of time and money really does work. God immediately began opening doors for her, putting her in touch with people who could help her with her new business venture and giving her clarity and healing in her relationship with her mother, who in turn bestowed a financial blessing toward her new business. Her mother even encouraged her own friends to support this woman with their financial blessings. As she discovered, when you speak your desires into the Universe, they shall come to pass.

Tithing provides a constant reminder of our connection to the Source from which all good comes. When you tithe with gratitude and appreciation, when you give thanks, you focus your attention on the Source and become open and receptive to receiving your rich, abundant supply.

Honor Yourself Enough to Stay the Course

God is with those who persevere.

— The Koran

Sometimes, honoring our commitments to ourselves and to the Source that supplies all good in our lives is simply a matter of having the courage of our convictions. We must honor ourselves enough to stay focused on our goal, to persevere no matter what.

> A woman had very negative feelings associated with tithes due to her religious upbringing but she decided to start tithing to see how it worked. She found someone that provided her with spiritual support and peace and immediately started tithing.
>
> After a few weeks she realized her financial situation was improving, although she could not identify how her financial situation could be improving, as she had not received any increase in income. She just felt better about her financial situation and herself.
>
> After a few months she stopped tithing. Sure enough, her financial situation changed and within a year she had amassed $15,000 in debt. She again decided to start tithing and immediately wrote a check for 10% of what she had in the bank and

157

once again began tithing 10% of her paycheck.
She felt wonderful and, after just a few days, she
sensed that things were looking up.

Even though her income had not increased,
she was again paying her bills and her money
seemed to be lasting longer than in the past.

We all must learn the benefits of tithing at our own pace
and we must come to our own expanded version of prosperity
in our own lives, even if we're surrounded by people who
practice the art of tithing. After many years of listening to me
talk about the joy of tithing, my dear friend Janet vibrantly
demonstrated that giving with faith and joy is an important
step to receiving greater good.

Janet wanted to tithe to her local homeless
shelter, but she felt her tithe would leave her
"almost" broke for a week. Eventually, she
stepped out in faith, saying, "God, you'll make
sure I'm taken care of if I tithe this amount." She
wrote her tithe check and that afternoon received
a new client. Every day since she wrote the check,
something new and wonderful has happened to
her and her business.

She vowed to never again put off her tithing
and vowed to tithe faithfully every month with an
open heart and a prayer of thanks.

A massage therapist who practices the art of
tithing on a daily basis rolls any missed tithes into
the next day's tithe. She has fun mailing out
checks, no matter how small, and every time she
does she gets another call for massage therapy.

A woman tithed and made her desire known
for increased prosperity in her flower shop. She

loves doing floral arrangements for weddings,
and was amazed at how many weddings she
booked in the month following her first tithe. She
received her increased prosperity by doing what
she loved.

How will you know when it's time to step out in faith?
When you begin to remember that everything is in divine order.
When you're willing to feel the fear and do it anyway. When
you're ready to commit to having a good time in your life—no
matter what expected or unexpected results occur.

Making the commitment to having a good time with your
tithes, in every area of your life, means letting go of your
expectations of the outcome. Yes, you may desire a certain
outcome. Simply affirm that this outcome *or something better* is in
store for you, and then step out in faith. Every mile is walked
one step at a time. A swing soars higher, one push at a time. All
journeys begin this way.

How do we learn to put one foot in front of the other?
How do we learn to push a swing at just the right time? Trial
and error. Not every attempt is perfect. Seek progress, not
perfection. Ask anyone who's jammed a finger pushing a swing
too soon, or felt their fingertips barely brush the back of the
person on the swing because they've pushed too late. Ask any
toddler who's taking those first tentative steps. It's all trial and
error.

But what keeps us trying? What keeps us moving forward
and waiting for the next opportunity to take those steps or to
push the swing again? Hope. Hope and a commitment to honor
ourselves by having a good time playing on the playground.

159

Life is your own personal playground. Make a commitment, starting today, to have a good time with the rest of your life.

Bless everything in your life, especially anything you pay money for. You will soon discover there is great joy in giving thanks for what your bills represent—and you will soon stop dreading the arrival of your mail or expenses that crop up.

When you sit down and write out the electric bill, spend some quality time actually thinking about what your money represents. It represents the electricity that keeps the fridge running, so you don't have to worry about your food spoiling and you can have ice cream with your children. It represents the air conditioning or heat that keeps your home comfortable. It represents the power to your computer that allows you to reach out across the world and meet new people and learn new things. What does your car repair bill really represent? It represents freedom to come and go to work as you please, to go for a drive to visit friends, be alone at the beach, get to the doctors, transport your kids in safety, and so on.

How much are those blessings really worth? The $2-$3 per gallon you pay for gas doesn't just pay for the fuel that gets you around. It also pays the taxes for smooth roads that provide you with a gentle drive, and road signs that get you where you're going (or help you get un-lost if you're like me!), and so on.

What are these pleasures really worth? If your electric bill is $150 this month, did you get $150 worth of enjoyment, peace of mind, serenity and fun out of your electricity? I usually find that the value I place on my enjoyment is ten times what I'm actually paying. The next time you pay for something, *joyfully* write out your check or hand over the money, and thank the Universe for all the gifts that bill represents. Like me, you may

160

find that paying your bills becomes just another form of tithing. Bless everyone you come into contact with. Bless them and see them receiving their heart's desires.

> A woman hated being at work because of two co-workers who constantly complained about everything. She began seeing her co-workers happily working in their right and perfect jobs—somewhere else. Within three months, both complaining co-workers had left to work somewhere else and her workplace once again became a joyful place to be.

Incorporate simple affirmations into your day, like *I see gold dust in the air!* (a good affirmation when springtime pollen flies everywhere!) or *Every day, in every way, I see my abundance growing and growing and growing, thank you God!* or *God is the source of my supply* or *I let go and trust the Universe to provide.* If you find your prosperity consciousness drifting off center, remind yourself that everything that is happening in your life is happening for a reason and that the reason something is happening is *always* for your highest good—even if you can't see the good in the reason.

Use a phrase like *Thank you, God!* whenever something happens in your life, no matter what it is. Other effective phrases include *It's all Good* or *This is for my highest good.*

Get a flat tire? *Thank you, God.* Get cut off in traffic? *Thank you, God.* Someone lets you into the flow of traffic? *Thank you, God.* Forget to return your library book? *Thank you, God.* Library fine gets forgiven? *Thank you, God.* Computer crashes? *It's all Good.* Someone gives you a check for $300? *It's all Good.* Someone gives you a bill for $300? *It's all Good.* Have a fight with a family member? *It's for my highest good.* Get praised at work? *It's for my highest good.* Get your car broken into? *It's for my highest good.*

No matter what happens, give thanks for the event and *know* that it is bringing you closer to where you're supposed to be. Even something tragic carries hidden blessings. When you are completely overwhelmed, use the phrase: *You meant this for evil, but God meant it for good.* Know that everything that happens in your life and everyone who comes into your life is here to help you heal, grow, and become the best you can be.

Turn tithing into an active game of thanksgiving. Actively seek out people who feed your spirit and tithe to them. Look for the times you smile or chuckle to yourself over something that you see, read or hear and immediately ask yourself: who can I thank for this gift? Give the first tenth of your income, give of your time, give of your talents, and give of your possessions, but above all else, give freely, willingly and joyfully. Remember the man who paid his bills instead of paying his $400 tithe? The Universe had quickly responded to the gratitude in his first tithe by opening up new and exciting channels of good for him. Divine flow was established, and he stepped into it effortlessly and was amply rewarded. But then he turned around and forgot to give thanks for the new prosperity that had manifest. He wasn't a good steward of the abundance that was being handed him, and suddenly the flow stopped. When it did, he became engulfed by fear.

When you find yourself faced with fear over a decision of whether to tithe or whether to pay a bill that's coming due, I encourage you to take the leap of faith, tithe and stay focused on reality: God is the Source of All Your Good. You'll quickly discover that your faith is more than amply rewarded.

A man was inspired to step out in faith and to begin sharing what God had given him. He was scared, because he was deeply in debt and didn't have enough to pay his necessary expenses, but he had faith. He could see many potential doors opening, and had faith that his good would appear, even though his prosperity had not yet manifested.

I shared with him this affirmation: *"I am fearless in letting money go out, knowing God is my immediate and endless supply."*

He wrote to me three months later to share some of the good news that was occurring in his life. He had made more money in the previous three months than he had ever done, and felt more joyful and open to new experiences. He had become more willing to go for what he wanted and more willing to spend money on things that helped him grow. When a month starts out slowly, he reminds himself that God is the source of all abundance and can give him what he has asked for, even if he doesn't know how.

This man began affirming that he was making at least $4,000 a month and by the end of the month he had come to within a couple hundred dollars of that goal. When he counted his gross abundance (not just the dollars he received), he found he was way above his goal.

Today, he is constantly receiving little gifts and signs of God's love and feels more in tune with the universe. He has paid off all his peripheral debts and now only has his main credit card debt to pay back. I am certain that within a year, he will be completely debt free.

When you step out in faith and tithe in the face of apparent lack, you show the Universe you can be a good and faithful steward of the abundance that's already present in your life. Once you give thanks with your tithe, be still for a moment. Then stay open and receptive to the doors that open, stepping out in faith that God will provide you with all that you desire. Honor yourself. Set your clear intentions of what you want, make those desires known and step out in the faith that what you seek will be given to you in divine timing in a way that is for your highest good.

You'll discover that tithing out of a sense of joy, thankfulness and gratitude breathes new life into your giving. As a result, you will find yourself straying from the activity of tithing less often. See tithing as a joyful opportunity to express your thanks, and good will flow into your life effortlessly. If you view tithing as an effort, or an obligation, what you receive will also be received with effort and a sense of obligation. Life was never meant to be a struggle. We don't have to live with disappointment.

Give with joy, give with faith and give with love. Tithe in all ways and then watch and see if God doesn't expand you and pour *you* out—a blessing that cannot be contained (see my audiotape lecture on the **Truth About Giving and Receiving** for more about this concept). All around you, channels of good will open that allow you to accomplish even more than you'd originally desired in your life.

> Within 13 months, a women went from
> having over $13,000 in unsecured debt to being

completely debt free and achieving her dream of
a fabulous California vacation. She didn't think it
was possible, yet she was willing to hold onto the
idea that it *might* be possible. And it *was!*

Many people have shared career-related success stories
that have brought them closer to their desire of having jobs
that allow them to follow their true life purpose. It's wonderful
to see the power of tithing at work in a collective way, creating
an economy where people get paid to do work that feeds their
souls. When you give to channels that feed your soul, the
Universe naturally responds by providing you with your own
overflowing helping of soul food.

A woman occasionally experienced clients
who appeared to not respect her time and energy
or forgot to pay their bills in a timely fashion.
When she let go of her attachment to the situation, and let go of the client, she often discovered
a better client waiting in the wings. She would
never have had time, space or energy for the new
client if she hadn't let go of the old client.

This woman was experiencing the effects of the Divine
Law of Prosperity. When you release something from your life
that no longer serves you—whether it's a person, a debt, or the
outcome to a situation—release it with thanksgiving for the
role it played in your life. In this way, you honor and value your
true inner worth, just as you honor and value your spiritual
Source when you release your tithe. You're honoring the fact
that the situation you have found yourself in was there for a
reason and may no longer be necessary in your life. By honoring

and valuing yourself in this way, and eliminating whatever is restraining your time and energy with resentments and negative thinking, you create a vacuum for new good, in the form of new abundance to come to you.

It's often hard to walk away from situations that no longer feed your spirit, particularly when they're in the form of money providers. Do not view money providers as the source of your security. They are merely one channel that provides you with a connection to the Source of your true, infinite security.

> A woman began walking away from good-paying opportunities that weren't feeding her soul. As she took this leap of faith, she had to confront her fears about money and security, and where the income would come from to replace the potential income she'd just released. In doing this work, she opened up the possibility for new, greater opportunities to arrive—and they began arriving right on schedule.

When you let go of something that's not working and you make room for something new to appear without any knowledge of what that might be, you're stepping out in faith. You're stepping out in the belief (consciously or unconsciously) that there will be something better. Many people stumble upon this prosperity principle of creating a vacuum for more good to flow into (because nature abhors a vacuum). They usually get so fed up with being treated as "less than" that they throw up their hands and walk away from a situation, with an attitude of "I don't know if what I truly deserve is out there but I know that this ain't it." They walk away from jobs, clients, relationships, you name it, and then find that what they truly deserve appears in their life like magic.

Do not get so focused on trying to change the problem into what you think you *do* deserve that you miss the good when it appears in your life. Do not be so fearful of making a mistake that you fail to act when what you truly deserve appears. You may be familiar with the phrase: "If it's too good to be true, it probably is." This is almost certainly the number one reason people miss the good in their lives. Do not use the above phrase to justify not taking action in the face of fear. Do not use it to avoid the hard acts of everyday courage that will propel you toward success.

Giving thanks through the art of tithing is the simplest way to achieve success in all areas of your life. It is simple, but it is not easy. Changing your thoughts is hard work; make no mistake about it. It is far easier to pick up the remote control and click on the television or engage in idle gossip bemoaning the fate of the world or others around you, than it is to sit quietly and consciously hold the thought that only good can come from a situation and that this good manifests to fill your desires, in divine timing. What's happening around you at any given time is merely what's happening. How you feel about those events is another matter.

Giving thanks through the art of tithing requires you to hold a consciousness of thankfulness in all that you do, all that you say and all that you think. Giving thanks through the art of tithing requires you to find the hidden blessing in every event and to give voice to that blessing. You are continually reaping the fruits of your words and your actions. As you sow, so shall you reap.

A woman who was moving to the United States tithed fearlessly, even though her only income was from a part-time teaching job. Her desire was for the right and perfect price for a plane ticket from her home in Spain to her new home in the United States. Not only did she manifest a $300 ticket during the prime travel season, she manifested gifts to pay for the deeply discounted ticket.

Measuring Your Success

When you measure your abundance in the actual cash that flows in your life, you wind up overlooking a great deal of the abundance in your life. In one 30 day period, I received the following: thousands of dollars worth of fantastic clothing, including a floor-length, fully-beaded, backless, emerald green evening gown; food; meals out; airline tickets; traveling accommodations; flowers; a free vacation; concerts; office assistance; more clothes (and fashion guidance!); a four-day Landmark Forum course; Mary Kay products; a fabulous drum; ice cream; spiritual counseling; a channeling session; gourmet meals; massages and original art. The list went on and on. This is an example of how the Universe will open up and support you when you step out in faith, perform your services with lovingkindness, let go of your attachment to the outcome, ask for what you desire and always give thanks for what you have received.

Even greater than the gifts you receive and the gifts you give will be the growth you will experience as a result of practicing the art of tithing. As you practice giving and receiving without attachments or expectations, you will notice that you are making fewer and fewer judgments.

During the month I received the above gifts, I had very little cash flow. If I measured my success by judging the appearance of my checkbook balance, I wasn't being very successful. The outpouring of abundance in my life was quite evident, however, when I focused on the big picture.

We carry around all these preconceived notions of what is success or failure, what is good or bad and what is right or wrong, because someone else taught us to believe these things. The truth is, everything that God created just IS. There is nothing that is good or bad, but that YOU make it so. There are only things and events. You make the judgment of what's good or bad based on your beliefs and assumptions.

Think about it. Think about a time when you heard music that didn't resonate with you. You immediately judged it as bad. You labeled it as off key, or nothing but noise, or untalented. You gave it a label: "bad music." Yet there are others who love that type of music. (Sometimes you may even extend your label to the people who love that music and say "they don't know good music.")

Consciously or unconsciously, you label everything. You label art, you label yard sale items. You label people's behavior and people's beliefs. You label experiences. For instance, we aren't born with a fear of dogs. Yet many children become afraid of all dogs at an early age. They believe dogs will hurt them because someone taught them to be afraid of dogs or someone reinforced this fear after the child was hurt one time by one dog.

Our words and actions are the most impressive teachers we have. Through our thoughts, words and actions, we teach children to be afraid or hate so many things. We teach children to hate bills, to be afraid of failure, to hate what they don't understand, to hate delays or things that don't turn out the way they expect them to turn out, to be afraid that their own talents and abilities won't be "good enough" to support them financially.

Fortunately, we can also use our thoughts, words and actions to teach children to embrace life. Realign your attitudes with the truth: Nothing is good or bad, but that we make it so. This enables you to tap into the limitless flow of abundance that's already readily available in your life. True prosperity—true, radiant abundance—starts with the knowledge that your thoughts make you a co-creator of the good in your life.

> A woman went home after tithing at my prosperity seminar and found $5 in the back pocket of her jeans as she was undressing. The next day, while pumping gas she received nearly $20 too much in change. The gas attendant was very thankful for her immediate correction of the error. By taking right action, she kept herself in the flow of abundance A few days later, she received a notice from the IRS that they were sending her $500. This woman also discovered with great appreciation, that her 14-year-old daughter already lives prosperity principles and vowed to learn from her child how to embrace and give thanks for the abundance in her life.

$$\Omega$$

A woman tithed once and within a week her income multiplied tenfold so that her new tithe was ten times her original tithe. The prospering power of 10, the tithe in action, once again!

Ω

A man wanted to manifest increased business for his engraving company. He went home the first night he tithed and received an order from a new client for eight plaques.

Ω

A full-time musician was continually faced with financial challenge and anxiety. She often found herself living 'hand to mouth.' One day, she decided to put on her 'faith' cap and chose to change her perspective about money. She began tithing and giving thanks for the abundance in her life. The more she chose to use the word 'challenge' instead of 'problem' when she spoke and thought about money, the more the money came to her. And it still does.

Ω

A woman stated her intention to fulfill a lifelong dream of visiting Mali, Africa and to get a great bargain on her airfare. After tithing for twelve weeks, what she had held in mind manifested on the day she'd set as a deadline. Before she left for her trip she was able to manifest an even better bargain. She is a shining symbol of the prospering power of tithing.

171

Don't Forget to Breathe!

"I can feel the magic floating in the air!"
— Faith Hill

Remember, tithing is like breathing. What's more natural than breathing? All the air you will ever need already surrounds you. You inhale, effortlessly, and air comes rushing in, time after time. But if you hold your breath and refuse to let the air in, you could suffocate. The air is there, but you believe you lack air because you choose not to let it in. What happens when you finally stop trying to hold your breath? You let go of the air you were holding onto and new, fresh air comes rushing in. Big gasping gulps of air come rushing in, more abundant, more pure, and carried more deeply into your lungs. This is what happens when you finally stop withholding your tithe.

In times of stress, it's easy to forget to breathe. Your breathing becomes rapid and shallow, or you exhale and forget to inhale again. Sometimes you need to consciously remember, or have someone remind you, to breathe. So it is with remembering that the substance of abundance is in your mind. So it is with remembering to tithe.

Sometimes you will forget to breathe it in. Sometimes you will forget to breathe in the abundance that surrounds you at all times. You can breathe substance deep into your mind with thoughts of abundance just as easily as you breathe air into your lungs. Sooner or later, breathing substance in through your thoughts and breathing substance out through your tithes will become as natural an activity as breathing air. When it does, you'll begin to manifest untold riches that will come to you in unimaginable forms. Don't be afraid to breathe in the abundance that is rightfully yours, and breathe out your thanks and gratitude.

Expanding your prosperity consciousness is as simple as expanding your lung capacity. The more abundance you make room for in your life, the more you will experience.

My dear friend (and fellow chocolate-lover) Beth once gifted me with a ticket to a sneak preview of the Oscar-bound movie, *Chocolat*, while I was visiting her in Manhattan. The strength of the main character, Vianne Rocher (played by Juliette Binoche), stuck with me. A wayfaring chocolatier, Vianne is repeatedly judged and found guilty of a myriad of sins in every situation she finds herself. Yet she has the courage of her convictions and the inner fortitude to stay the course and honor herself, even when the obstacles in her path seem insurmountable.

As one reviewer put it, Vianne "set off a confrontation between those who would keep life the same and those who would revel in their newly discovered taste for freedom." As you change and grow and begin to practice the art of tithing in all you do, the people around you may not always appear supportive. We are all human, and as humans, we dislike change, as a rule. Our natural inclination is to take action to prevent change from taking place. Do not be dismayed or disheartened when this happens. Stay the course. Be strong, be courageous in your convictions.

To achieve your goals, you must stay the course and be true to your heart's desire, no matter how many obstacles, no matter how many heartbreaks and heartaches and fears and setbacks get in your way.

As you wrestle with the angels that surround your past beliefs about tithing, and the beliefs others may have about tithing, fear not. The reality of the situation is that you are the beloved child of abundant, loving, giving Divine parents. You hold and nurture within yourself unique talents that will draw other people together. Follow your heart and help others heal. Do not allow your fears to hold you back from making the commitment to practicing the art of tithing, by giving thanks in every area of your life. You are worth it and you deserve it.

Epilogue

Every ending is a new beginning.

It is my fervent hope that this book has helped you gain a spiritual understanding of tithing as well as an intellectual understanding.

Knowing that tithing works and believing that you are giving thanks for the abundant good in your life when you tithe are two distinct entities.

I cannot take you into the land of spiritual understanding where your abundance awaits you. I can, however, tell you how to seek this land and I can even relate story after story of the treasures others have found in this land.

But you must undertake the journey for yourself.

You must step out in faith and prime your own pump.

I have given you all the tools I have. I have shown you the pump and provided you with a helping of spiritual food— use the spiritual inspiration contained in this book as your first cup of water. The rest is up to you.

You must find the courage to do what you think you cannot do, as Eleanor Roosevelt would say.

I wish you well on your journey, my friend.

For on-going inspiration, I encourage you to visit my website (www.ArtOfAbundance.com) and subscribe to my free e-zine, *The Art of Abundance.*

Paula Langguth Ryan
February 8, 2005

P.S. Please write and let me know how your life is unfolding for your highest good. I love receiving cards, letters, postcards and photographs from my readers. Correspondence can be sent to me at:

Paula Langguth Ryan
1121 Annapolis Road, Suite 120
Odenton, Maryland 21113
PaulaRyan@ArtOfAbundance.com
www.ArtOfAbundance.com